INTERNATIONAL
Herald Tribune
THE WORLD'S DAILY NEWSPAPER : iht.com

Reading the News

Pete Sharma

HEINLE
CENGAGE Learning™

Australia • Brazil • Japan • Korea • Mexico • Singapore • Spain • United Kingdom • United States

HEINLE
CENGAGE Learning

Reading the News
Pete Sharma

Publisher: Christopher Wenger

Director of Content Development:
Anita Raducanu

Development Editor: Sarah O'Driscoll

Associate Development Editor:
Jennifer Meldrum

Editorial Assistant: Bridget McLaughlin

Associate Production Editor: Erika W. Hokanson

Product Marketing Manager: Amy Mabley

Print Buyer: Mary Beth Hennebury

Project Manager: Howard Middle /
HM ELT Services

Contributing Writer: Tay Lesley

Compositor: Pre-Press Company, Inc.

Cover Designer: Rebecca Silber

Printer: West Group

Cover Image: © ZEX Photography/Thomson ELT

Library of Congress Control Number: 2006904669

ISBN-13: 978-1-4240-0381-5

ISBN-10: 1-4240-0381-4

Heinle
25 Thomson Place
Boston, Massachusetts 02210
USA

Cengage Learning is a leading provider of customized learning solutions with office locations around the globe, including Singapore, the United Kingdom, Australia, Mexico, Brazil, and Japan. Locate your local office at: **international.cengage.com/region**

Cengage Learning products are represented in Canada by Nelson Education, Ltd.

Visit Heinle online at **elt.heinle.com**

Visit our corporate website at **cengage.com**

Photo Credits

page 7: © Photos.com/RF
page 11: © IndexOpen/RF
page 15: © Photos.com/RF
page 19: © IndexOpen/RF
page 25: © IndexOpen/RF
page 37: © IndexOpen/RF
page 47: © Franck Robichan/
International Herald Tribune
page 55: © Photos.com/RF
page 59: © Photos.com/RF
page 59: (top left) © Photos.com/RF,
(top right) © Photos.com/RF,
(bottom left) © IndexOpen/RF,
(bottom right) © IndexOpen/RF

page 60: (top) IndexOpen/RF, (center)
© IndexOpen/RF, (right) © IndexOpen/RF
page 65: © IndexOpen/RF
page 69: © Photos.com/RF
page 73: © IndexOpen/RF
page 83: © IndexOpen/RF
page 100: (top left) © IndexOpen/RF
(top right) © IndexOpen/RF, (bottom left)
© IndexOpen/RF, (bottom right)
© IndexOpen/RF
page 105: © Thomas Crampton/International
Herald Tribune
page 109: © IndexOpen/RF

Printed in the United States of America
4 5 6 7 11 10 09 08

Contents

NEWS AND FEATURES

1 > NEWS

People primarily read the newspaper for . . . news! News can be a *breaking* story, where the facts are changing moment by moment, or it can involve a recent event in a long-running story, where it is important for the reader to know the background. With *hard* news the most important factor is that it is read today—we rarely pick up yesterday's newspapers to read about current news.

Think about an article you have read in the newspaper recently. Why was it in the news? Was it a breaking or long-running story? How important and significant was it?

2 > UNDERSTANDING NEWS ARTICLES

2a   News stories answer the following questions:

What happened?

When did it happen?

Who was involved?

Where did it happen?

Why / how did it happen?

These questions are answered briefly in the first or second paragraph of the article, as the purpose of the article is to elaborate on the answers.

2b   Using the IHT Web site.

Go to the *International Herald Tribune* (IHT) Web site at www.iht.com and find a news story that interests you. Complete the following grid.

Story headline	
What	
When	
Who	
Where	
Why / how	

3 > FEATURES

Feature articles are less "time-dependent." In other words, they are not so tied to an exact moment in time, but address contemporary areas of interest to the reader.

Before reading a feature, it is useful to ask yourself what you know about the subject. In doing so, you will do the following:

- Predict vocabulary which may occur in the article; this can help reduce the "processing load"—the amount of new information you need to cover in order to understand the text.
- Think about how much you know about the background to the story. If you know very little, you will look for this information in the article. If you know a lot, you might *skim* over parts of the text which provide readers with this information.
- Identify questions you want the text to answer; this will give you a "reason for reading" the text.

4 > UNDERSTANDING FEATURE ARTICLES

The purpose of a headline is to get the reader's attention. A good headline should make the reader curious and provoke interest in the article.

4a **Look at the two headlines below, taken from the four articles in this section.** What do you think each article is about?

A hunger for English lessons

As smoke clears, tobacco maker opens lounge

4b **Here are some useful questions you can ask yourself before reading the articles in this section.** Add more points before reading the articles.

	BACKGROUND NOTES	QUESTIONS
A hunger for English lessons	English lessons are popular / expensive in my country. It can be nerve-wracking speaking English in front of native speakers.	Why are people "hungry" to learn English?
As smoke clears, tobacco maker opens lounge	More and more countries are banning cigarette smoking in public places	Which tobacco company? What "lounge" is opened, and why?

4c **Look at the other two articles used in this section.** With a partner, discuss what you think the article will be about.

4d **With a partner, predict what vocabulary you might need for all four articles.**

A hunger for English lessons

1 **Focus on language learning.** Which expressions reflect best your own experience of learning English? Compare your answer with a partner.

memorization of vocabulary lists	learning grammar rules
reading texts	watching videos and listening to cassettes
fluency and conversation classes	meeting with English-speaking people
having a native-speaking teacher	having a non-native-speaking teacher

2 **When you learn to speak English, which is more important?** Put an X on the line at the position which best reflects your view. Compare and discuss your answer with a partner.

SPEAKING ACCURATELY ←————————————→ SPEAKING FLUENTLY

TARGET LANGUAGE ONLY ←————————————→ USE OF YOUR NATIVE LANGUAGE IN CLASS ALLOWED

3 **The language of business.** Define the following words.

competitiveness _____

natural resources _____

exports (n) _____

corporate giants _____

> READING FOCUS

Focus on the newspaper: COMPARING AND CONTRASTING

Newspaper articles are "cohesive." This means the text flows logically—it is not a series of statements written one after the other. Among the most important cohesive devices are "connectors." Some of these are for making comparisons, or for contrasting two different situations.

1a **Study the list of contrasting connectors.** What purpose does each connector have?

Although	Nevertheless
However	On the one hand… on the other hand
Despite the fact that	In spite of

1b **Find the connectors in paragraphs 9, 10, 11 and 13 and <u>underline</u> them.** Consider why they are being used and what is being contrasted in each case.

A hunger for English lessons

By Choe Sang-Hun

1   Kim Hyo Jin, a timid junior high school student, stood before her American teacher fidgeting. The smiling teacher held up a green pepper and asked in clear, enunciated English: "What is this?"

2   "Peemang!" the South Korean teenager blurted out, then covered her mouth with a hand as if to stop—too late—the Korean word that had left her mouth.

3   Mortified, she tried again. Without looking the teacher in the eye, she held both her hands out and asked, this time in English: "May I have green pepper?"

4   Kim took the vegetable with a bow, and darted back to her giggling classmates—beaming and feeling relieved that she had successfully taken a small first step toward demolishing what South Koreans consider one of their biggest weaknesses in global competitiveness: the fear of speaking in English to Westerners.

5   Kim was among 300 junior high school students going through a weeklong training in this new "English Village." Built a few kilometers from the western border with North Korea, the government-subsidized language camp is, at 280,000 square meters, or 3 million square feet, the largest of its kind in the world, officials say.

6   The complex—where the motto is, "We produce global Koreans!"—looks like a minitown scooped up from a European country and transplanted into this South Korean countryside dotted with pine groves, rice paddies and military barbed-wire fences. It has its own immigration office, city hall, bookstore, cafeteria, gym, a main street with Western storefronts, police officers and a live-in population of 160 native English speakers. All signs are in English, the only language allowed.

7   Here, on a six-day immersion course that charges students 80,000 won, or $82, apiece, pupils check in to a hotel, shop, take cooking lessons and make music videos—all in English. There are language cops around, punishing students speaking Korean with a fine in the village currency or red dots on their village passports. To relieve the stress, the authorities do permit students to speak their native tongue a few times during their stay, usually at mealtimes.

8   Across South Korea, the English Villages are sprouting up. Ten are already operating, with more on the way. They represent the latest big push in South Korean parents' multibillion-dollar-a-year campaign to give their children a leg up in conquering English skills.

9   Despite the fact that South Korea has very few natural resources, it realized early on that it must push exports and produce high-quality work forces. Education is an obsession. Mastering English is a nationwide quest from kids to office minions in corporate giants like Samsung and Hyundai.

10   "It's funny because Koreans know English," said Jeffrey Jones, former president of the American Chamber of Commerce in Korea who heads the Paju complex. "They can read, probably better than I can. However, they have trouble speaking."

11   Although they spend a lot of time learning English, when many Koreans see a Westerner coming their way on the street, they detour or run away.

12   South Korea has become one of the most aggressive countries in Asia at teaching English to its citizens. Outside the school system, parents are paying an estimated 10 trillion won a year to help their children learn English at home or abroad.

13   Nevertheless many college graduates falter in chats with native speakers. South Korean officials are often accused of grouping together in international conferences, afraid to mix with native English speakers. That, linguists say, is a result of a national school system that traditionally stresses reading and rote memorization of English grammar and vocabulary at the expense of conversation.

14   In Korea University of Seoul, 30 percent of all classes are now in English. Speaking English with a native accent has become a status symbol.

Read the complete article and answer the questions below.

1. What problem did Kim Hyo Jin have?

2. Who funds the English village?

3. Why is Korea so "aggressive" when it comes to encouraging students to speak English?

4. What happens in the English village if students speak Korean?

5. What do Korean delegates usually do at international conferences?

> VOCABULARY WORK

LEARNING TIP: Writers often use colorful verbs to enrich and enliven an article. Usually these verbs have a more easy-to-understand equivalent, or synonym. Recognizing these words can expand your receptive vocabulary, and help you to enjoy the article more.

1a Focus on verbs. Match the verbs in the first box with a corresponding verb in the second box which has a similar meaning. What is the difference between the verbs?

sprout up	knock down
enunciate	pronounce
chat	feel pleased
dart back	talk
giggle	smile
beam	flee
blurt out	return
falter	grew up
demolish	laugh
feel relieved	say
run away	stumble

1b Complete the sentences with a word from Exercise 1a. You may need to change the form of the verb.

1. She was a great athlete but she _____ at the last hurdle and fell.

2. What a fool. He got drunk and just _____ the secret!

3. He hated living with his new foster parents and he _____ from home.

4. He spends all evening _____ on MSN Messenger.

5. They finally _____ that old warehouse on Silver Street—it just had to go!

> EXAM PREPARATION TASKS

1 Look at the passage again. Match the article's sub-headings below with the appropriate paragraphs from the article. One sub-heading will not be used.

_____1. paragraphs 1–5   A. English Villages

_____2. paragraphs 6–8   B. Importing Foreigners

_____3. paragraphs 9–12   C. Identifying the Root of the Problem

_____4. paragraphs 13–14   D. Afraid to Speak English

                                   E. An Obsession with Speaking English

2 Look at the squares in the paragraphs below. Circle the square that indicates the best place to add the **bolded** sentence.

1. **They are from many different English-speaking countries so no one accent is dominant.**

   ■ The complex—where the motto is, "We produce global Koreans!"—looks like a minitown scooped up from a European country and transplanted into this South Korean countryside dotted with pine groves, rice paddies and military barbed-wire fences. ■ It has its own immigration office, city hall, bookstore, cafeteria, gym, a main street with Western storefronts, police officers and a live-in population of 160 native English speakers. ■ All signs are in English, the only language allowed. ■

2. **The English language business is booming.**

   ■ Across South Korea, the English Villages are sprouting up. ■ Ten are already operating, with more on the way. ■ They represent the latest big push in South Korean parents' multibillion-dollar-a-year campaign to give their children a leg up in conquering English skills. ■

3. **The Korean government spends millions on English education.**

   ■ Nevertheless many college graduates falter in chats with native speakers. ■ South Korean officials are often accused of grouping together in international conferences, afraid to mix with native English speakers. ■ That, linguists say, is a result of a national school system that traditionally stresses reading and rote memorization of English grammar and vocabulary at the expense of conversation. ■

> DISCUSSION PROMPTS

1. In your opinion, will English remain the most important global language?

2. Re-read the description of the English village. Would you like to study there? Why / why not?

3. What is the most effective way of learning a language?

Have foreign MBA, will travel in Chinese business

> PRE-READING TASKS

1 **Which of the following business terms and concepts are you familiar with?** Explain them to a partner.

MBA program	a business school	a state-owned enterprise
an entrepreneur	management consulting	a multinational company
recruiter	supply and demand	business network

2 **How important do you think English is to become a successful business executive?** Which of the following statements do you agree with most?

1. It's not important. Many successful executives only deal with their local market.

2. It's important. Many business concepts are developed in the US, and training is in English.

3. It's very important. Successful executives today work in a global environment.

> READING FOCUS

Focus on the newspaper: THE FIVE W'S

A good way to approach an article and extract the key information is to ask yourself the five *Wh*-questions: *What? Where? When? Why? Who?* This key information can usually be found in the first and second paragraphs of an article.

1 **Read the article and complete the missing information below.**

What happened?	
Where?	
When?	
Why?	
Who?	Hellmut Schütte:
	Steve Mullinjer:
	Jevan Soo:

2 **Which paragraphs did you find this information in?**

Have foreign MBA, will travel in Chinese business

By Sonia Kolesnikov

1   Insead, one of the top European business schools, based in Fontainebleau, near Paris, opened an Asian campus in Singapore several years ago. This autumn, if all goes according to plan, it will take an additional step into the Asian market, with the introduction of an executive MBA program in China, offered jointly with Tsinghua University, of Beijing.

2   "The Chinese believe very strongly that China is unique and therefore they should learn something on China in China," Hellmut Schütte, the dean of the Singapore campus, said in an interview.

3   "That is understandable," he continued. "American business schools are dominating the field with their way of business thinking, which is all very interesting but is not always applicable back in China's state-owned enterprises. But at the same time, students appreciate they need to learn about global practice. This is why many local schools are now offering joint programs with international business schools. Students can get the best of both worlds."

4   The program may make life easier for Steve Mullinjer, a recruiter in Shanghai for Heidrick & Struggles, an international executive search firm based in Chicago. "Foreign-trained executives that can prove they can adapt their learned skill sets to the local market are in rare supply, but in great demand," Mullinjer said.

5   MBA-holders with international exposure are increasingly in demand in China, a country that has created plenty of successful, self-taught entrepreneurs, but few with much experience of Western-style best-management practices.

6   As Chinese companies face increasing international competition in their own backyard, while simultaneously taking on the outside world, the limitations of their senior executives' understanding of Western practices can often weigh them down.

7   A few years ago, many Chinese executives would have jumped at the opportunity to study abroad, but now they are hesitant to leave, for fear that they will not only lose touch with the country's fast evolving economic realities, but also lose precious business contacts and networks.

8   The management consulting firm McKinsey estimates that Chinese companies, given the global aspirations that many nurture, will need 75,000 leaders who can work effectively in global environments over the next 10 to 15 years, compared with the 3,000 to 5,000 that they have now.

9   "When you add on top of that the hiring needs of multinationals doing business in China, you can imagine the vast demand for executive talent in the country," said Jevan Soo, McKinsey's manager of Asia-Pacific recruiting, in Shanghai.

10   In the short-term, companies are coping through a variety of mechanisms, including continuing to bring both Chinese and non-Chinese expatriates from overseas, and developing local hires from entry-level positions to managerial roles.

11   "However, the long-term solution will require a shift in the Chinese education system to increasingly emphasize the practical skills and the English language skills that global companies require," Soo said.

12   Foreign universities have been quick to pick up on the trend, and in the last couple of years joint-executive education programs have flourished.

13   Insead's intended partner in its executive MBA program, Tsinghua, one of the top Chinese universities, already offers an international MBA program in collaboration with the Massachusetts Institute of Technology's Sloan School of Management. Graduates of the program earn a Tsinghua MBA and a Sloan certificate.

14   But, Schütte said, the Insead-Tsinghua qualification would be the first dual-degree executive MBA offered by top international and Chinese business schools in China.

15   "Most multinational firms are still hiring in relatively small numbers at Chinese MBA schools as compared to their hiring levels at U.S. and European MBA schools," Soo, of McKinsey, said. "However, it is only a matter of time before Chinese schools close this gap."

> COMPREHENSION WORK

Read the article and answer the questions below.

1. What was Insead's previous involvement in Asia?

2. Do you agree with the view expressed by the dean of the Singapore campus?

3. How will companies cope in the short term?

4. What, according to the article, will need to change in the long term?

5. What is so special about the Insead-Tsinghua collaboration?

> VOCABULARY WORK

LEARNING TIP: Collocation is an important feature of English. Collocation is the way words combine with other words to form strong and frequent "word partnerships."

1 **Focus on collocations.** Create a word partnership from the article, using the words in the box below.

firms	market	demand	practices	environment	program	practice

1. joint _____

2. Western _____

3. multinational _____

4. local _____

5. vast _____

6. global _____ _____

2 **Complete the sentences below with a phrase or collocation from Exercise 1 above.**

1. There is a _____ for executives who have local and international experience.

2. It's a small shop that sells specialty items for the _____.

3. McDonald's is, arguably, the most famous example of a successful _____.

4. Japan and Korea have a _____ for engineering students of either country.

5. We can no longer think of producing goods for a local economy. In today's world, we must always think about how our products will sell in a _____.

6. Chinese business students like going to Harvard in order to learn about _____.

> EXAM PREPARATION TASKS

1   Circle the letter of the best answer.

1. Which of the following statements would the author agree with?

    A. A Chinese businessperson doesn't need knowledge of American best-practice.

    B. Studying overseas is the best way for a Chinese businessperson to get ahead in the field.

    C. Chinese business schools also need to emphasize English language skills.

    D. There is a great demand for people with Chinese MBA degrees.

2. Why do the Chinese want a European business school in China?

    A. It is too expensive to travel to Europe.

    B. They feel the American schools are too restrictive in their enrollments.

    C. The uniqueness of Chinese makes it hard for them to study overseas.

    D. They feel they need to stay in China to network.

3. Why does the author mention both MIT and Insead in paragraphs 12 and 13?

    A. to demonstrate how the two universities will compete

    B. to contrast what the two schools are offering

    C. to exemplify the domination of American thinking

    D. to refute the need for additional business schools

2   Look at the squares in the paragraph below. Circle the square that indicates the best place to add the **bolded** sentence.

> **It is important for Chinese managers to understand the laws and protocol in China.**
>
> "That is understandable," he continued. "American business schools are dominating the field with their way of business thinking, which is all very interesting but is not always applicable back in China's state-owned enterprises. ■ But at the same time, students appreciate they need to learn about global practice. ■ This is why many local schools are now offering joint programs with international business schools. ■ Students can get the best of both worlds." ■

> DISCUSSION PROMPTS

1. Would you like to study in another country? Discuss your answer with a partner.

2. "American business schools are dominating the field with their way of business thinking." Do you agree with this?

3. What makes a good executive? List three key qualities. Compare and discuss your list with a partner.

As smoke clears, tobacco maker opens lounge

> PRE-READING TASKS

1   Answer the following questions about your smoking habits.

1. Are you a smoker?

2. If yes, how long have you been smoking? If not, have you ever smoked?

3. What do think about different tobaccos? (cigarette, pipe, cigar)

4. Have you ever rolled your own cigarette?

2   How do you feel about smoking? Circle all adjectives that apply and discuss your answers with a partner.

Smoking is…

glamorous   nasty   sociable   fun   dangerous
    relaxing   attractive   disgusting   elegant   silly

> READING FOCUS

Focus on the newspaper: DIRECT AND INDIRECT QUOTATION

When writing articles based on comments from a variety of people, reporters use both direct and indirect quotation. This helps to vary the style.

1a   Find the comments by the people below. Check whether direct, indirect, or both direct and indirect quotation is used.

	Direct	Indirect	Both
1. Brian Stebbins (para. 4, 5, 11)	_____	_____	_____
2. Those who fought for the smoking ban (para. 6)	_____	_____	_____
3. Bronson Frick (para. 7)	_____	_____	_____
4. Sean Fahey (para. 8)	_____	_____	_____
5. Several anti-smoking advocates (para. 9)	_____	_____	_____
6. William V. Corr (para. 9)	_____	_____	_____
7. Richard A. Daynard (para. 10)	_____	_____	_____
8. Bob Kittrell (para. 11 & 12)	_____	_____	_____

1b   Of the individuals named in Exercise 1a, who is pro-smoking, anti-smoking, or neutral?

Pro-smoking	Anti-smoking	Neutral

As smoke clears, tobacco company opens lounge

By Monica Davey

1 The room is lined with vintage ashtrays, delicate lighters, matches and pens shaped like cigarettes. The scent, naturally, is of smoke.

2 Chicago's smoking ban took effect this week, but it was hard to know that from inside the gleaming lounge along Milwaukee Avenue in a hip neighborhood on the North Side. Here, under glass, are thick jars of tobacco—Oriental Rose, The Empress, The Earl—poured lovingly into white smoking papers by tobacco's answer to the coffee shop barista.

3 At the very moment smokers around Chicago were learning not to light up on train platforms, in sports stadiums and in some restaurants, a subsidiary of R. J. Reynolds Tobacco Company was preparing for the grand opening on Thursday of its answer to the smoke-free set: the Marshall McGearty Tobacco Lounge, what its creators intend to be the nation's first upscale, luxury lounge dedicated to the smoking of cigarettes, especially a new R. J. Reynolds variety.

4 The timing, Brian Stebbins, a senior marketing director at R. J. Reynolds, said, was purely coincidental. And the shop, he insists, does not fall under the city's new ban since it fits the exempt category of a "tobacco retail store," even though it also sells alcoholic drinks, cheese plates and espresso drinks.

5 "That's incidental," Mr. Stebbins said, as he wandered the lounge on Wednesday, pointing out the dark wood, the marble bar, the cozy seats by a fireplace. "This is about a select, super premium brand of cigarettes, just like what we've seen with the super premium tier of beer, wine, chocolate and pastries. It's about elegance and having fun."

6 Not so much fun for those here who fought for the smoking ban—one of the growing number of such restrictions around the country—who said they found the lounge puzzling, disconcerting and possibly illegal.

7 Some antismoking advocates nationally said they worried that the Chicago store might mark a new front in the tobacco industry's efforts to market their products as glamorous, particularly to a young, cutting-edge audience, despite efforts by the industry to comply with a 1998 settlement agreement with scores of states that limits advertising. "It's trying to get an 18-to-25 demographic here, to make smoking seem desirable, attractive, like a secret club," said Bronson Frick, associate director for Americans for Nonsmokers' Rights, a group based in Berkeley, Calif.

8 Regardless, on Wednesday afternoon, Sean Fahey, 29, wandered by, stood at the smoking bar and sucked deeply and quizzically on his first Oriental Rose—a step up, he said, from his plain old Camels. "More and more places like this are sure to open up," Mr. Fahey said. "No one is going to stop smoking because of a ban, but maybe people can start treating cigarettes like this more like alcohol—the kind of thing you savor."

9 Several antismoking advocates said the lounge, indeed, seemed to comply with the legal terms of the settlement, though some said they wondered whether it was truly meeting the intent of the agreement. "Glamorizing tobacco use will encourage young people who are smokers to continue doing so, and it will encourage some young people who don't smoke to do so—just because it's a glamorous, upscale place," said William V. Corr, executive director of the Campaign for Tobacco-Free Kids. "The question of whether this appeals to youth is a factual question we will have to watch."

10 But Richard A. Daynard, a law professor at Northeastern University and president of the Tobacco Control Resource Center, said he was not bothered by the lounge, mostly because he believes the idea will not work. "It's a gimmick," he said. "I certainly would be surprised if it's still in business five years from now. The problem is that their clientele is not this, but mainly working class and poor people."

11 For his part, Mr. Stebbins said he had not considered whether such smoking lounges might move elsewhere too. "I'm focusing on Chicago right now," he said. Across the room, Bob Kittrell, 45, sat smoking.

12 "This is my place now," said Mr. Kittrell, who lives nearby. "It's the only place around that I can drink coffee and read the papers and smoke my cigarettes anymore." He was, in fact, smoking his own cigarettes, a box of ordinary Camels, but said he might try the Marshall McGearty mix sometime.

> COMPREHENSION WORK

Read the article. Then read the statements and decide if each is a fact (F) or an opinion (O).

_____ 1. The Marshall McGearty Tobacco Lounge sells food and drink as well as tobacco.

_____ 2. It's coincidental that the lounge opened soon after a smoking ban began to be enforced.

_____ 3. The opening of the lounge upset some anti-smoking advocates.

_____ 4. Tobacco companies are trying to market smoking as glamorous.

_____ 5. People should start treating tobacco use like alcohol consumption.

_____ 6. Because it's such an attractive place, the lounge will be successful.

_____ 7. Richard Daynard thinks that the tobacco lounge is a gimmick.

_____ 8. The lounge allows people to bring in their own cigarettes.

> VOCABULARY WORK

1   The article contains a number of words related to the topic of smoking. Find several examples for each of the following:

things smokers use   **types of tobacco**   **what smokers do (verbs)**
        ashtray

> **LEARNING TIP:** Paired adjectives. Pairing adjectives with similar meanings can add effect.
> For example, *She spoke in an excited, dramatic voice* is stronger than *She spoke in an excited
> voice* although the meaning of the two adjectives is similar.

2a   A number of paired adjectives appear in the article. Scan the article for the missing adjectives below. Write the things that they refer to and the paragraph number they are found in.

Paired Adjectives	Thing referred to	Paragraph
1. _____, luxury	_____	_____
2. _____, super premium	_____	_____
3. puzzling, _____	_____	_____
4. desirable, _____	_____	_____
5. _____, upscale	_____	_____

2b   Which two adjectives you found for Exercise 2a have a similar meaning?

> EXAM PREPARATION TASKS

1 **Below is the first sentence of a summary of the article.** Complete the summary by writing the letters of three answer choices that best express the *main ideas* from the article.

> **At the same time that Chicago banned smoking in public, the R. J. Reynolds company opened a new smoking lounge downtown in the city.**

- _____
- _____
- _____

A. People in Chicago can no longer smoke on train platforms, stadiums and restaurants.

B. The lounge is aimed at an upscale market for discerning tobacco smokers.

C. The tobacco industry's biggest clientele is traditionally the upper class.

D. There is some debate about whether the lounge is legal with the new smoking laws.

E. Anti-tobacco groups fear the new lounge glamorizes smoking to younger people.

F. The lounge is only open to people over 18 years old.

2 **In the blanks below, write the correct form of the verb in parentheses.**

When anti-smoking advocates (1) _____ (ask) about their opinions regarding the lounge, several (2) _____ (say) the lounge, indeed, seemed (3) _____ (comply) with the legal terms of the settlement. However, some said they wondered whether it (4) _____ (meet) the true intention of the agreement. "Glamorizing tobacco use will encourage young people who (5) _____ (be) currently smokers (6) _____ (continue) doing so, and it may (7) _____ (encourage) some young people who (8) _____ (not smoke) to do so—just because this lounge (9) _____ (seem) like a glamorous, upscale place," (10) _____ (say) William V. Corr, executive director of the Campaign for Tobacco-Free Kids.

> DISCUSSION PROMPTS

1. Does the tobacco lounge described in the article sound like an attractive place to you? What are the most appealing features of the lounge?

2. Do you think the tobacco lounge is likely to be successful? Why or why not?

3. Agree or disagree with the following, and discuss your reasons with a partner: "The selling of upscale tobacco should be treated like the selling of other luxury goods, like chocolate or fine pastries."

Secret wealth vs. 'for richer, for poorer'

> PRE-READING TASKS

1   **Look at the words in the box below and check that you understand the meaning.** With a partner, write the words under the correct category. Which words belong to more than one group?

court	divorce	counseling	assets	tax	therapy	debts
vows	estate	accounts	legal	spouse	wealth	inherit

LAW	PSYCHOLOGY	PROPERTY	MARRIAGE	FINANCE

2   **Is divorce common in your country?** In general, what are people's attitudes towards divorce?

> READING FOCUS

Focus on the newspaper: RECOGNIZING PATTERNS

It is easier to process an article if you notice the patterns in the text. Often the writer uses *linking words* or *discourse markers*. These show the connection between what has already been said and what is going to be said.

1a   **Scan the text and highlight or <u>underline</u> the following words.**

Instead (para. 1)	But (para. 2)	On the whole (para. 8)
Moreover (para. 9)	To sum up (para. 14)	

1b   **Look at the following uses of discourse markers.** Match the words above to their use:

1. emphasizes a contrast _____

2. gives a counter-argument to a previous point _____

3. generalizes _____

4. concludes _____

5. introduces additional information _____

1c   **Read paragraphs one and two again.** What was the situation and what action was taken? Complete the following information.

PARAGRAPH 1
situation ———————— Instead ————————▶ *action*

_____   _____

PARAGRAPH 2
situation ———————— But ————————▶ *action*

_____   _____

Secret wealth vs. 'for richer, for poorer'

By Sharon Reier

1   When Linda, a social worker in the New York area, received a significant chunk of money after her mother died, she did not divulge the amount to her husband of 15 years. Instead, she set up separate accounts earmarked for the education of their son and daughter.

2   Worried that her marriage would flounder once her children left home, Madame M., the wife of an Asian industrialist, bought an expensive apartment in central Paris to prepare as a possible escape hatch. The money she used had been inherited from her father. The marriage survived. But a decade later, her husband and children still don't know about the Paris property.

3   Such behavior is perfectly legal. But the people who engage in it are reluctant to use their full names for fear of destabilizing their families.

4   The classic marriage vows may urge "for richer, for poorer," but concealing financial activities from a spouse is hardly a new strategy. Over a century ago in his play "A Doll's House," Henrik Ibsen used the device of a wife's secret loan to unveil the dynamics of an unhealthy marriage.

5   But in an age when divorce and serial marriages have become commonplace, when many women are entering marriages earning large sums and such assets are an increasing component of family wealth, it is not just billionaires like Ronald Perelman, president of Revlon, and Donald Trump who are concerned about protecting what is his, what is hers and what is theirs.

6   While prenuptial agreements and even postnuptial agreements are increasingly being used to set boundaries, in the end, who gets what depends on legal jurisdiction, sound financial planning, national traditions and the psychological state of the marriage.

7   Common sense may dictate that since most countries require income tax returns signed by both spouses, husbands and wives should at least know what the other is earning. But this is not necessarily so, experts in marriage counseling and family law say.

8   At Relate, the largest couples counseling charity in Britain, each couple is given an exit evaluation after a course of therapy. One question they are asked is, "Do you know how much your partner earns?" On the whole, people say no, said Denise Knowles, a counselor at Relate, whose clients come from all levels of society.

9   In England and Wales, prenuptial agreements often are not recognized in court. Moreover, in contrast to most U.S. states or France, where the Napoleonic Code governs marital property, England and Wales stipulate that all assets that are brought into the marriage or inherited can be considered part of the marital estate and can be claimed by an unhappy partner, or even spouses and children from previous unions.

10   "Many people do not understand this and have a very expensive prenuptial agreement drawn up in the United States," Maizels said. "They move to England, and later the English court will not recognize it."

11   Napoleonic law provides for a legal form of marriage called a *séparation de biens,* which stipulates no community property and therefore releases each spouse from responsibility for his partner's debts. "Usually it is advisable to choose this regime if the husband has risky business activities," Lapeyre said. In the United States, a prenuptial agreement would be necessary to guard one spouse from the other's debts.

12   increasingly concerned about the assets they brought into the marriage. Women with high earnings capacity, she said, are "often influenced by their mother's situation."

13   "Either she never had her own money and she couldn't do things," Maizels said, "or she had wealth, but lost it supporting a previous partner, or worse, a partner's previous relationship."

14   To sum up, while a financial crisis may force a couple to pull together, realizing a fortune may cause a couple to squabble about things that were not debatable before. The differences can lead to separate lives, and sometimes to divorce.

> COMPREHENSION WORK

Look at the following questions and circle the letter of the best answer.

1. The writer suggests that concealing financial activities from a spouse is:

   a. difficult   b. a new strategy   c. long-practiced

2. The success of a prenuptial agreement depends on:

   a. the man's income   b. a range of factors   c. the health of the marriage

3. Inheriting a fortune can lead to:

   a. a more stable marriage   b. arguments   c. a financial crisis

> VOCABULARY WORK

1a   Focus on prepositions. Match the phrases in the first column with the words in the second column. Select the correct connecting preposition from the box below. All the expressions can be found in the article. One of them has been done for you.

to	up	from	from	~~from~~	about	about	by

1. she did not divulge the amount   _____   a. the other's debts

2. she set   _____   b. a spouse

3. inherited   _____   c. protecting what is his

4. concealing financial activities   _____   d. separate accounts

5. concerned   _____   e. things that were
                                                                            not debatable before

6. influenced   _____   f. their mother's situation

7. squabble   _____   g. her father

8. to guard one's spouse ⟶ _from_   h. her husband

1b   Create your own sentences with some of the expressions in exercise 1a.

> EXAM PREPARATION TASKS

1 **Look at the underlined pronouns in the paragraphs below.** Connect the pronoun to the word or phrase it refers to by circling the word or phrase and drawing a line between the pronoun and its referent.

1. With the number of successful women entrepreneurs and high-level professionals rising, Maizels said women were increasingly concerned about the assets they brought into the marriage. Women with high earnings capacity, she said, are "often influenced by their mother's situation."

2. At Relate, the largest couples counselling charity in Britain, each couple is given an exit evaluation. One question they are asked is, "Do you know how much your partner earns?" Many people say no, said Denise Knowles, a counsellor at Relate, whose clients come from all levels of society.

3. Concealing financial activities from a spouse is hardly a new strategy. Over a century ago in his play "A Doll's House," Henrik Ibsen used the device of a wife's secret loan to show an unhealthy marriage.

2 **Use the words in the box to complete the sentences.** Some words will not be used.

because	either	however	instead	moreover	or	since	when	while

1. _____ a social worker received an inheritance from her mother, she did not tell her husband how much she received.

2. _____ she never had money of her own, or she lost her wealth supporting someone else.

3. _____ financial crisis may force some couples to pull together, for other couples, telling a spouse about a secret stash can lead to divorce.

4. In England, prenuptial agreements are often not recognized in court. _____, all assets brought into a marriage are considered communal property.

5. She did not tell her husband. _____, she set up a separate account for her children.

> DISCUSSION PROMPTS

1. If two people marry, should they share everything? Or, should one person be allowed to keep part of their wealth in their own name? What should happen if one person in a marriage inherits property?

2. In today's society, are prenuptial agreements a good idea? Are they recognized in your country?

3. Should unmarried couples have the same rights as married people?

OPINION

1 > EDITORIALS AND COMMENTARY

The opinion pages of a newspaper cover controversial areas that are in the news, such as politics or religion. The writer will often use very strong language because their job is to give an opinion.

The editorial team members of the *International Herald Tribune* write two or three short articles which express their views and opinions. Such views are often political, and newspapers become known for their political sympathies, or declaring themselves to be "independent" or free from political opinion.

1a Look at the list of jobs below. Do you know what kind of work they do on a newspaper? Discuss your ideas with a partner.

Publisher	Business Editor	Marketing Director
Managing Editor	Technology Editor	

1b All editorials start dramatically as the writer has a limited space in which to express and defend a forceful opinion. Match the three editorial headlines below with their opening sentences.

_____ 1. Making the UN work

a. If there ever was a moment in the American debate over immigration when presidential leadership was urgently needed…

_____ 2. The oceans resurface

b. Management and budget reform surely lacks the sizzle of other subjects typically debated at the United Nations…

_____ 3. An immigration impasse

c. Despite the extensive studies demonstrating the poor health of America's coastal waters…

1c Vocabulary check. Check that you know the meaning of the following words:

a-political	biased	unbiased	politician	spokesperson

2 > OPINION

2a When you read a text, you will process the information and view it from your own point of view. Before reading an opinion article, it's a good idea to think of your own view. Among the things to consider when reading an opinion article are:

Does the writer use an emotional argument or a logical argument?
Is the article balanced or does the writer express his or her own view?
Is the article supported by details, facts and evidence?

When you have finished reading an article, consider if the article changed your views.
Try drafting a reply to the article with the opposite viewpoint.

2b Look at the statements below. All of these ideas have appeared in the *International Herald Tribune.* You will encounter some of these opinions in this section. Mark the closest number (1–5) to your own opinion. Discuss your answers with a partner.

1 = Strongly disagree   2 = Disagree
3 = Not sure / don't know   4 = Agree
5 = Strongly agree

	1	2	3	4	5
Capital punishment is wrong					
Smoking should be banned in public places					
People should be free to say whatever they like					
Nuclear power plants are potentially dangerous					
Globalization is bad for developing countries					
Men will always earn more money than women					
Fast food restaurants should take responsibility for encouraging obesity					

3 > THE ARTICLES

This section contains four articles. Read the headlines below. Which controversial areas do they address? What is your opinion on these topics? Discuss your ideas with a partner.

Nuclear power industry feels the wind at its back

Women's work / The wages of equality: A world of unfinished business

Managing globalization: If it's here to stay, what do we do now?

Chances a low-fat diet will help? Slim and none

Nuclear power industry feels the wind at its back

> PRE-READING TASKS

1   **Match each term with its definition.** What else do you know about these terms?

1. fossil fuels	a. a chemical material and a basic material used for nuclear technology
2. radioactive waste	b. a place where nuclear power is generated
3. nuclear reactor	c. waste material given off during a nuclear reaction
4. uranium	d. natural resources such as oil, coal and natural gas formed in the ground over millions of years

2   **What do you know about the following nuclear accidents:** Chernobyl and Three Mile Island? Mark each of the following statements either (C) or (3M):

1. Accident happened in April, 1986 _____

2. Accident happened in March, 1979 _____

3. Accident happened in Pennsylvania, USA _____

4. Accident happened in the Ukraine _____

5. The worst accident in nuclear history _____

6. The US stopped building power plants after this event _____

7. About 200,000 people were evacuated and resettled _____

8. No one was evacuated _____

3   **Energy sources.** Which of the following sources of energy are used in your country? How popular are they?

gas	oil	coal	wind	water	nuclear power	solar power

> READING FOCUS

Focus on the newspaper: DEVELOPING AN ARGUMENT

While it is important to keep a balanced view, some writers like to put across their own view and build an argument in favor of something. Understanding the development of an argument is vital in processing a text.

1   **Read the introduction to the article below.** How do you think the article is going to develop? Do you think the writer is going to be for or against nuclear power? Why?

> SHUNNED for years because of its potentially disastrous effects on the environment, nuclear power has been showing signs of a renaissance in recent months, benefiting from concern over high energy prices, rising demand and the ecological impacts of fossil fuels.

2   **Scan the text.** What phrases can you find that help the reader understand the argument?

Nuclear power industry feels the wind at its back

By Barbara Wall

1   Shunned for years because of its potentially disastrous effects on the environment, nuclear power has been showing signs of a renaissance in recent months, benefiting from concern over high energy prices, rising demand and the ecological impacts of fossil fuels.

2   When a reactor at the nuclear power plant at Chernobyl in southern Ukraine blew up on April 26, 1986, exposing millions of people across Europe to radiation, plans for new nuclear reactors were scrapped around the world. But sentiment toward the industry appears to be shifting as safety and economical production of electricity from nuclear plants reaches all-time highs.

3   Advocates of nuclear power point to its comparatively low fuel costs. It is argued that, although expensive to build, nuclear plants are relatively cheap to run. Taking into account back-end costs such as the fabrication of uranium and the management of spent radioactive materials, the total fuel costs of a nuclear power plant are typically about one-third of those of a coal-fired plant and about one-quarter of those of a gas combined cycle plant, reported the World Nuclear Association in London.

4   Environmentalists are among the most vocal opponents of nuclear power, yet paradoxically it could be one of the cleanest fuels available. John Ritch, director-general of the World Nuclear Association, said that atomic energy was the only source that could meet the world's rising energy needs without threatening the environment. Unlike gas, oil and coal, nuclear plants do not emit carbon dioxide, which is thought to be a major contributor to global warming.

5   The United States has emerged as one of the strongest proponents of nuclear power. A recent task force has come out in favor of nuclear energy.

6   No new nuclear reactors have been built in the United States since March 28, 1979, when a plant at Three Mile Island in Pennsylvania malfunctioned and released radioactive gas into the atmosphere.

7   In France, the only Western European country that has had an active nuclear power construction program, sites have been designated for new power reactors and construction is expected to resume in a few years.

8   In other regions of the world, opposition to nuclear power has not stopped policymakers from building new reactors. About 30 power reactors are currently being constructed in 11 countries, notably China, Japan and South Korea, according to the Nuclear Energy Institute, based in New York.

9   Assuming that the pundits are correct and the nuclear power industry is on the brink of a renaissance, the suppliers of its raw material—uranium—could be the first to benefit.

10   "The uranium market has been a difficult place to be during recent years," said Steve Kidd, head of strategy and research at the World Nuclear Association. "The price of uranium has been depressed because of oversupply in the market; as a result, mining companies have been unable to invest in new facilities.

11   "There is light at the end of the tunnel and the mining companies are hopeful that prices will improve, but it will be some time before uranium suppliers see an improvement to their bottom lines."

12   Uranium enrichment is a critical step in transferring the naturally occurring form of the element into a fuel for reactors.

13   A revival of interest in nuclear power appears to have boosted interest in the nuclear generators.

14   Three Mile Island and Chernobyl may be fading memories, but the disposal of radioactive waste remains one of the industry's most controversial issues.

15   Robin Jeffrey, chairman of British Energy, said that while the technical and safety issues have largely been resolved by the creation of improved waste repositories, political issues also need to be addressed.

16   "The nuclear power industry needs to get much better in presenting the environmental case for nuclear power and its crucial role in combating global warming and pollution," he said. "The industry needs to demonstrate that any new build program has a genuinely robust case. Given the progress made in recent years, another four years could mark a significant milestone for the industry."

> COMPREHENSION WORK

Read the complete text. Complete the grid with "pro" and "anti" nuclear power arguments.

Pro nuclear power plants	Against nuclear power plants

> VOCABULARY WORK

1a Word formation. Complete the grid below with the missing words.

Noun	Adjective	Verb
	disastrous	——
benefit		
		to economize
		to react
construction		
	opposite	
strategy		
controversy		——
generator		
		to waste

1b Now complete the following sentences with words from the grid.

1. Disposal of radioactive waste remains one of the industry's most _____ issues.

2. With the rise in fuel prices, we really need a new way to _____ power.

3. He was surprised to find so much _____ to his idea. He thought it would be accepted easily.

4. Turn off the light—it's so _____ to leave them on in an energy crisis!

5. The general was known for his _____ brilliance; he out-maneuvered his opponents on the battlefield.

6. The poor really _____ from his generosity and kindness.

2 Vocabulary expansion. Find words or expressions in the article from the following definitions:

1. to deliberately avoid something (para. 1) _____
2. to decide not to continue with something (para. 2) _____
3. the amount of money spent to build something (para. 3) _____
4. experts (para. 9) _____
5. at that point in time when something is about to happen (para. 9) _____
6. a new interest in something (para. 9) _____

> EXAM PREPARATION TASKS

1 **According to the information in the article, determine if the statements below are true, false or not given in the article.** Next to the sentences, write T, F, or NG.

_____ 1. Environmentalists traditionally support clean nuclear power over polluting fossil fuels.

_____ 2. Generating power from a nuclear plant is the cheapest form of energy.

_____ 3. Nuclear power plants are costly to construct.

_____ 4. The last nuclear power plant built in the U.S. was on March 28, 1979.

_____ 5. Asian governments stopped building nuclear power plants because of public opposition.

_____ 6. France has the most nuclear power plants in Europe.

_____ 7. Uranium prices have been steadily increasing over the years.

_____ 8. Uranium has to be enriched in order to use it for fuel.

_____ 9. Nuclear power plants have found new ways to dispose of radioactive waste.

_____ 10. Nuclear power is the primary source of power in Asia.

2 **Below is the first sentence of a summary of the article.** Complete the summary by writing the letter of three answer choices that best express the *main ideas* from the article.

Nuclear Power is enjoying a comeback.

- _____   - _____   - _____

A. A new interest in nuclear power means there is more interest in disposing of radioactive waste.

B. For years after Chernobyl and Three Mile Island, nuclear power was shunned as being dangerous.

C. Many Asian countries are currently constructing nuclear power plants.

D. Radioactive waste is not as objectionable as it once was.

E. The United States is assembling a nuclear energy task force.

F. Advocates are pointing out that nuclear power can be cleaner and cheaper than fossil fuels.

> DISCUSSION PROMPTS

1. Are you "for" or "against" nuclear power? Justify your argument. Predict the opposite argument and refute it.

2. "The disposal of radioactive waste remains one of the industry's most controversial issues." How, in your opinion, should radioactive waste be disposed?

3. If nuclear power were abolished in your country, which two energy sources would you recommend and why?

Women's work / The wages of equality: A world of unfinished business

> PRE-READING TASKS

1 **What is discrimination?** Insert vowels in the following words which are used with, or form collocations with, the word "discrimination":

g__nd__r discrimination   to discriminate __g __ __ nst   __g__ discrimination

s__x__ __ l discrimination   r__l__g__ __ __ s discrimination   r __ c __ __ l discrimination

2 **Write definitions for the following terms, in your own words.** Use a dictionary if necessary.

the gender wage gap _____

"gender politics"   _____

wage inequality   _____

3 **Where does your own country lie on the following scales?** Mark an X on the line. Compare your answer with a partner.

WOMEN'S WAGES ARE HIGH   ⟵⟶   WOMEN'S WAGES ARE LOW

THERE ARE MANY WOMEN IN THE WORK FORCE   ⟵⟶   WOMEN HAVE A VERY "TRADITIONAL" ROLE IN SOCIETY

MATERNAL LEAVE IS GENEROUS/CHILD CARE FACILITIES ARE GOOD   ⟵⟶   THERE IS LITTLE MATERNAL LEAVE/POOR CHILDCARE FACILITIES

> READING FOCUS

Focus on the newspaper: READING FOR DETAILS

In some articles, there are many details and facts. Understanding the details will help you understand the article better.

As you read, answer the questions.

1. What types of economies have drawn more women into the work force?

   _____

2. What is the main reason women get paid less than men?

   _____

3. What are some social policies governments could look at to help lower this gender gap?

   a. _____   b. _____   c. _____

   d. _____   e. _____

4. What does a free market do to wage inequalities? _____

Women's work / The wages of equality: A world of unfinished business

By Erika Kinetz

1   In the United States, there are more women in the work force at higher levels than in any other country in the world—and they still make less than their male counterparts. In Sweden, women's wages are high, but their role in the work force remains relatively traditional. In Germany, maternal leave is generous, but many women drop out of the work force once they have children. In Japan, the gap is not just in wages but also in the basic structure of the way men and women are employed.

2   In good times and in bad, women's wages have become an increasingly important component of household income and consumer spending. The shift toward service-based economies in the industrialized world has favored women in the work force—one reason they have poured into the labor market over the past three decades.

3   But what they find once they get there differs considerably throughout the developed world. That has less to do with gender politics than it does with macroeconomics, and it results—somewhat surprisingly—in women still being paid less than men in most places and for most jobs.

4   The reasons for this persistent inequity are complex, and they vary with geography. In many places, discrimination in education and hiring is responsible for a diminishing fraction of the gender wage gap.

5   These days, having and raising children seems to be a much bigger drag on a woman's earning power. Many women choose to interrupt their careers, working part-time or temporarily dropping out, to raise children. Such decisions can permanently disrupt earning power.

6   To the extent that discrimination contributes to the gap between men's and women's wages, the gender wage gap is a drain on productivity. And that, economists and labor experts say, could spell big trouble for a global economy struggling to shake off the past and cope with the challenges of the future.

7   Today, narrowing the gender wage gap is less a matter of empowerment than of economics, and getting women into the work force means paying attention to a host of social policies, like parental leave, taxes, and child care, as well as corporate attitudes and the practices they reinforce.

8   There has been progress, particularly in narrowing the gender wage gap. According to the Organization for Economic Cooperation and Development, in the late 1990s, the latest period for which broadly comparable global data are available, the gender wage gap was narrowest in Belgium, France, Sweden, and Italy, where full-time female workers earned 83 to 90 cents for each $1 earned by men, and broadest in Japan, Austria, and Spain, where full-time female workers earned 63 to 71 cents per male-earned dollar.

9   The United States, which brims with egalitarian pride, sits near the middle of the pack.

10   And left largely to its own devices, the free market has increased wage inequality. According to OECD data, wage inequality has remained relatively unchanged throughout much of Europe and in Japan over the last two decades, while it has increased in the United States. In the late 1990s in the United States, the wages earned by the doctors, lawyers, and high-level executives at the 90th percentile of the earnings distribution were 4.5 times higher than the wages earned by the domestics and burger flippers at the 10th percentile. In Sweden they were 2.2 times as high and in France and Germany three times as high.

11   Despite the head wind of wage inequality, women's wages have closed in on men's faster in the United States than anywhere else in the developed world.

12   Outside the United States, the gender wage gap has narrowed more slowly. For one thing, real wages for men haven't stagnated as they have within the United States; also, some economists say American women, in general, are better qualified and have made deeper inroads into traditionally male professions.

13   Among developed nations, Japan is an outlier. Despite women's high levels of education and experience, Japan has the highest gender wage gap in the developed world. According to the International Labor Organization, women in Japan earned, on average, 65.3 percent of men's salaries in 2001, up from 63.1 percent in 1997.

14   "There are sound economic reasons why governments have a case for intervening and making it attractive to more parents that they engage in paid work." There is no utopia. Each system has its own strengths and weaknesses. Sweden is often held up as a model nation, but it too has its drawbacks. There is no one right answer for how to most efficiently incorporate women into the work force.

> COMPREHENSION WORK

Choose the best option for each question.

1. The shift toward service-based economies in the industrialized world has been <u>bad / good</u> for women.

2. The wage gap has <u>more / less</u> to do with economics than gender politics.

3. The gender wage gap in the USA is narrow / broad / nor broad nor narrow.

4. Wage inequality is highest in <u>the USA / Germany / Sweden</u>.

5. The free market economy <u>benefits / does not benefit</u> women.

6. Outside the USA, wages have <u>increased / decreased</u> in real terms.

> VOCABULARY WORK

1a Match a word in the first column with one from the second column to create collocations taken from the article.

Noun–Noun		Adjective–Noun	
1. household	a. gap	6. global	f. world
2. consumer	b. force	7. maternal	g. structure
3. wage	c. spending	8. corporate	h. leave
4. gender	d. income	9. basic	i. attitudes
5. work	e. politics	10. developed	j. economy

1b Complete the sentences with a word from Exercise 1a.

1. In many companies, only 15 percent of the _____ _____ are women.

2. In Sweden, fathers commonly stay at home when a baby is born, although _____ _____ is more common.

3. It is very hard to change _____ _____ as employers usually worry about women taking time off to look after the family.

4. The rise in _____ _____ means it is very useful for women in households to generate an income.

5. Japan has the highest gender _____ _____ in the _____ _____.

2 Vocabulary expansion. What do the following terms mean?

1. macroeconomics _____

2. utopia _____

3. empowerment _____

4. drawbacks _____

> EXAM PREPARATION TASKS

1   Decide which statements are true for each country according to the article. Write the number of the true statements under the correct country. Two choices will not be used.

Statements	Countries
1. This nation has the best wages for women.	United States
2. Women make less money because they are less qualified.	•
3. The wage difference between men and women is the greatest.	•
	_____
4. As a nation, they talk big about equality between the genders.	Japan
5. Women are better qualified than men in traditional roles.	•
6. Men and women are employed differently.	•
	_____
7. This nation has the most women in higher professional positions.	Sweden
8. Women remain in traditionally female roles even though the possibility to make money is better than most countries.	•
	•

2   Circle the letter of the best answer.

9. Women's wages have become an _____ important component of household income.

   A. increasing

   B. increasingly

   C. increased

   D. increase

10. Narrowing the gender wage gap is less a matter of empowerment _____ of economics.

    A. than

    B. more

    C. as

    D. instead

11. Many women choose to interrupt their careers, working part time or temporarily dropping out, _____.

   A. for raising children

   B. than raise children

   C. to raise children

   D. raising children

> DISCUSSION PROMPTS

1.   Why do you think that women continue to earn less than men?

2.   Do you agree that women should always be paid the same as their male counterparts?

3.   Do you think there are still some "traditionally male professions" disappearing? How is society changing in respect to attitudes towards women?

Managing globalization: If it's here to stay, what do we do now?

> PRE-READING TASKS

1a In your opinion, is globalization basically a good or a bad trend?

1b List below as many positive and negative effects of globalization that you can think of.

Positive effects	Negative effects

2 Do you think it's possible to stop or slow down globalization? Why or why not?

> READING FOCUS

Focus on the newspaper: FOLLOWING A TREND

Newspapers often report on important economic, social or political trends. These trends involve complicated issues, and they may be controversial. People frequently disagree about whether they are good or bad, how important they are, and if they will continue in the future. All of these points need to be made clear to the reader.

1 **Scan the article for several effects of globalization.** Look only for actual changes, not just people's reactions to them. Write these below.

2 **Read the following viewpoints on the effects of globalization.** Decide whether each statement is positive (+), negative (–), or neutral (0).

1. ___ It influences the decisions that people make every day.

2. ___ It allows big companies to exploit workers in poor countries.

3. ___ It helps the world use its resources more efficiently.

4. ___ It has become so rapid that the labor force can't adjust to it.

5. ___ It creates winners and losers.

6. ___ It helps raise living standards in the developing world.

7. ___ It's impossible to predict how it will affect people in the future.

8. ___ It creates and destroys industries too quickly.

Managing globalization: If it's here to stay, what do we do now?

By Daniel Altman

1 Two decades have passed since the word "globalization" started showing up with any frequency in discussions of business and economics. At first, the focus was on Western companies' trying to compete with cheaper, sometimes better imports from Japan, South Korea, China and other countries. It was a straight fight: The battle lines were drawn along each country's borders.

2 Later on, things became more complex. Asian companies started designing and assembling products in the West. Western companies opened up new fronts by sending jobs abroad—not just in manufacturing but in service industries as well.

3 At the turn of the millennium, there was a lot of talk about whether globalization was a Good Thing or a Bad Thing. One side argued that it allowed big, multinational corporations to exploit workers in poor countries to pad their profit margins. The other side retorted that the expansion of these corporations into the developing world offered the best hope for raising living standards. One side complained that globalization was creating and destroying industries too quickly for the labor force to adjust. The other side answered that these shifts were rapidly improving the world's ability to use its resources efficiently.

4 Now it's pretty clear that globalization, be it good or bad, is an Unavoidable Thing. Rather than dealing with the problems of globalization head-on, it can be tempting to try to slow the process. Yet that's likely to postpone the problems, not solve them. Unless every country simultaneously decides to close its borders to commerce, migration and financial transactions, globalization will continue. Tariffs exist, of course, as do restrictions on foreign workers and foreign investment. But as technology for moving goods, people and information improves, globalization will accelerate.

5 How and why this is happening is well-trodden territory. Moreover, arguing about whether it's good or bad has become something of a simplistic activity. There are clearly winners and losers, and they're identified every day through layoffs, profit figures and the cash registers of retail stores carrying ever-wider selections at ever-lower prices.

6 The more relevant question now is how to manage the transition to a more globalized world. In theory, the gains of the winners in trade always outweigh the costs to the losers. So how can those gains be distributed so that everybody wins, at least a little bit?

7 People are making decisions every day that change the impact of globalization on their lives. Parents choose whether to pay for extra language lessons for their children. The chief executive in a dying industry weighs how much his company should invest in researching new products. A government minister tries to figure out how to keep her country's brightest scientists from moving overseas.

8 Yet it's not easy to plan for the future without knowing what the future will look like. Back in the 1980s, Americans were encouraging their children to learn Japanese. Now, Chinese is the language of choice. Solar-powered cars were all the rage, then electrical hybrids. In the next decade, fuel cells may take over. Though India still watches as hundreds of its brightest graduates head to the United States every year, more and more are staying home to start their own businesses.

9 The ground-level challenges require flexible solutions. Developing specific skills, inventing specific technologies or passing specific laws to fit the circumstances of the moment may not be enough.

10 It may be more important to develop skills that help you to pick up more skills, to invent technologies that set the stage for generations of innovation, and to pass laws that open the door to several different kinds of regulation—in other words, to create a platform for flexible decision-making in the midst of rapid changes.

11 Education, pension rules, intellectual property laws, tax policy, research spending, job training and the financial system—all of these areas are feeling the effects of globalization.

12 The integration of the global economy is making every single topic more complex. But each one is also involved in the solutions to those big challenges.

13 With that knowledge in hand, a few more winners may appear on the battlefield of the global economy.

> COMPREHENSION WORK

Each of the sentences below summarizes one of the paragraphs in the article. Read the article and write the number of the paragraph next to the best summary. Not all paragraphs have a summary below.

_____ 1. Globalization cannot be avoided; in fact, it is likely to accelerate.

_____ 2. It's impossible to know what changes globalization will bring.

_____ 3. The debate over globalization began with discussions about cheap imports.

_____ 4. There's little point in talking about whether globalization is good or bad.

_____ 5. The most effective way to prepare people for globalization is to teach them to "learn how to learn."

_____ 6. Around the year 2000, people debated the merits of globalization a lot.

_____ 7. Individuals constantly make decisions in their own lives in response to globalization.

> VOCABULARY WORK

1a Focus on the language of money and business. Scan the article for the missing words in these phrases.

1. big, _____ corporations.

2. ever-wider _____ at ever-lower _____.

3. Asian companies started designing and _____ products.

4. the _____ of the winners in trade always outweigh the _____ to the losers.

5. intellectual _____ laws.

6. not just in _____ but in _____ industries as well.

7. pad their _____ margins.

8. the best hope for _____ living standards.

1b Complete the sentences below. Use the correct form of the words you wrote in Exercise 1a.

1. The company is investing last year's record _____ in new machinery.

2. This is a good time to buy—before the government _____ interest rates again.

3. The retail _____ of that computer has been reduced; it's now only $300.

4. The main _____ for most businesses is employee salaries.

5. Last year the Swansons built a house on their _____ in the mountains.

6. If you want a better _____, you need to go to a bigger store.

7. Telemarketing doesn't make an actual product; it's an example of a _____ industry.

8. It's sometimes cheaper to make machine parts in one country and _____ them into the finished product in another.

> EXAM PREPARATION TASKS

1   Circle the letter of the best answer.

1. Which of the following statements would the author most likely agree with?

   A. Globalization should be viewed as a battlefield with winners and losers.

   B. Flexibility will probably be the most important skill for survival in the future.

   C. One way to better manage the losses associated with globalization is to slow it down.

   D. World leaders need to consider choices like language education, research and tariffs.

2. How does the author make the point that globalization is unavoidable?

   A. by detailing arguments in favor of expanding globalization

   B. by giving examples of past failed attempts to prevent globalization

   C. by showing how tariffs, laws and economies are complicated without globalization

   D. by proposing an impossible world-wide requirement to stop globalization

2   Circle the letter of the words or phrases below that best complete the paragraph.

Two decades have passed since the word "globalization" started showing up. (1) _____, the focus was on Western companies' trying to compete with imports from Asia. The battle lines were drawn along each (2) _____ borders. (3) _____, things became more complex. Asian companies started designing and assembling products in the West. At the turn of the century, there was a lot of talk about whether it was a good thing or a bad thing. (4) _____ it's pretty clear that globalization is an unavoidable thing.

1.	A. Now	B. First	C. At first	D. Therefore
2.	A. country	B. countries	C. country's	D. countries'
3.	A. Finally	B. Later on	C. Moreover	D. Second
4.	A. Now	B. Then	C. Lastly	D. In conclusion

> DISCUSSION PROMPTS

1.   Has reading this article made you think differently about globalization? In what way?

2.   The article raises a question which it doesn't actually answer: "In theory, the gains of the winners in trade always outweigh the losers. So how can those gains be distributed so that everybody wins, at least a little bit?" Why doesn't the article provide an answer? How would you answer it?

3.   Agree or disagree with this statement: "If all tariffs on imported goods were removed overnight, the world would soon become a more prosperous place." Discuss the statement with a partner.

Chances a low-fat diet will help? Slim and none

> PRE-READING TASKS

1   Match the medical term with its definition.

_____ 1. a stroke

_____ 2. insulin

_____ 3. chronic disease

_____ 4. cholesterol

_____ 5. diabetes

a. substance in blood; too much causes heart disease

b. medical condition due to lack of insulin and too much sugar in the blood

c. condition which often causes loss of ability to speak, and move certain muscles

d. serious and long-lasting disease

e. substance produced by the body which controls level of sugar in blood

2   Which expression(s) best describe you and your lifestyle? Discuss your answers with a partner.

I eat a low-fat diet ☐

I exercise regularly ☐

I eat a healthy diet ☐

I smoke ☐

I eat healthy foods ☐

I rarely exercise ☐

I never diet ☐

I smoke occasionally ☐

I eat a lot of fatty food ☐

I never exercise ☐

I go from diet to diet ☐

I don't smoke ☐

> READING FOCUS

Focus on the newspaper: LOOKING FOR EVIDENCE

When reading an opinion article it is important to follow the structure of the argument. This includes looking for evidence, identifying counter-arguments and recognizing bias. The writer may use certain "marker phrases" which signal that the article is going to change direction, or present an opposite point of view.

1a   Look for phrases that indicate a widely held belief or personal opinion. Underline these phrases in the text. Notice the transition between differing opinions.

1b   Below are eight arguments from the article. First, label which paragraphs these eight arguments come from. Second, match each argument (1–4) with its counter-argument (a–d). The first one has been done for you.

1. Largest diet study showed low-fat diet does not reduce the risk of cancer or heart disease.
    paragraph(s): _____1–3_____

2. Investigators believe it is best to eat less fats and eat more grains and fruits and vegetables.
    paragraph(s): _____

3. Some people caution that we can't always control our chances of getting a disease by watching what we eat.
    paragraph(s): _____

4. It is a widely held belief that too many carbohydrates cause weight gain.
    paragraph(s): _____

a. People think it is still okay to eat fats as long as they are the "right fats."
    paragraph(s): _____

b. Scientists believed for years that diet determined our chances of getting sick.
    paragraph(s): _____

c. One doctor thinks the diet study is inaccurate because it did not reduce fat enough and was not long enough.
    paragraph(s): _____5_____

d. Others think a low-fat diet will help people lose weight naturally.
    paragraph(s): _____

Chances a low-fat diet will help? Slim and none

By Gina Kolata

1   The largest study ever to ask whether a low-fat diet reduces the risk of getting cancer or heart disease has found that the diet has no effect.

2   The $415 million federal study involved nearly 49,000 women aged 50 to 79 who were followed for eight years. In the end, those assigned to a low-fat diet had the same rates of cancer, heart attacks and strokes as those who ate whatever they pleased, researchers reported Wednesday.

3   "These studies are revolutionary," said Dr. Jules Hirsch, physician in chief emeritus at Rockefeller University in New York City, who has spent a lifetime studying the effects of diets on weight and health. "They should put a stop to this era of thinking that we have all the information we need to change the whole national diet and make everybody healthy."

4   The results, the study investigators agreed, do not justify recommending low-fat diets to the public to reduce their heart disease and cancer risk. The investigators added that the best dietary advice was to follow federal guidelines for healthy eating—less saturated fats and trans fats, more grains and more fruits and vegetables.

5   Not everyone was convinced. Some, like Dr. Dean Ornish, a longtime promoter of low-fat diets and president of the Preventive Medicine Research Institute in Sausalito, California, said that the women did not reduce their fat to low enough levels or eat enough fruits and vegetables. He also said the study, even at eight years, did not give the diets enough time.

6   Others said that diet could still make a difference, at least with heart disease, if people were to eat the so-called Mediterranean diet, low in saturated fats like butter and high in oils like olive oil. The women in the study reduced all kinds of fat. But the Mediterranean diet has not been subjected to a study of this scope, researchers said.

7   Barbara Howard, an epidemiologist[1] at MedStar Research Institute, a nonprofit hospital group, and a principal investigator in the study, said people should realize that diet alone is not enough to stay healthy.

8   "We are not going to reverse any of the chronic diseases in this country by changing the composition of the diet," Howard said. "People are always thinking it's what they ate. They are not looking at how much they ate or that they smoke or that they are sedentary."

9   Except for not smoking, the evidence for advice on what makes a healthy lifestyle is largely indirect, Howard

said. Most medical re-searchers agree, however, that it also makes sense for people to eat well, control their weight and get regular exercise.

10   Others cautioned against being too certain that any particular diet would markedly improve health and noted that whether someone developed a chronic disease might not be entirely under their control—genetics also matters.

11   In this case, the diet study addressed a tricky problem. For decades, many scientists have said, and many in the public have believed, that what people eat determines how likely they are to get a chronic disease. But that has been hard to prove.

12   There is a common belief that Americans get fat because they eat too many carbohydrates. The idea is that a high-carbohydrate, low-fat diet leads to weight gain, higher insulin and blood glucose levels, and more diabetes, even if the calories are the same as in a higher-fat diet. That did not happen in the study.

13   Others have said the opposite: that low-fat diets enable people to lose weight naturally. But again, that belief was not supported by the data in the study.

14   As for heart disease risk factors, the only one affected was LDL cholesterol, which increases heart disease risk. The levels were slightly higher in women eating the higher-fat diet, but not high enough to make a noticeable difference in their risk of heart disease.

15   Although all the study participants were women, results should also apply to men.

---

1. epidemiologist: someone who studies infectious diseases

> COMPREHENSION WORK

Read the summary of the article and correct any mistakes you find.

This article describes the largest study ever to ask whether a low-fat diet reduces the risk of getting cancer or heart disease. It found that diet has little effect. The study followed nearly 49,000 women aged 50 to 79 for five years. On the whole, the results justify recommending low-fat diets to the public in order to reduce heart disease and cancer risk. It stands to reason, scientists argue, that what people eat determines how likely they are to get a chronic disease, and this has been relatively easy to prove. The debate about the effectiveness of dieting rages on and on. Furthermore, given that this study focused on women, further studies are needed to assess the effects on men.

> VOCABULARY WORK

LEARNING TIP: Many nouns and verbs have exactly the same form (e.g. a convict / to convict). It is useful to mark the stress on words (e.g., a CONvict [n.] / conVICT [v.]). Practice saying these words to yourself.

1a Nouns and verbs. The same or different? Mark the following V, N or both. If the word is a verb, write the noun. If the word is a noun, write the verb. Look at the examples. Note: sometimes there is more than one noun.

EXAMPLE: death (N)...*die...*   apply (V)...*application...*   fund...*(V/N)...*

1. diet _____	5. study _____	9. effect _____	13. investigate _____
2. reduce _____	6. difference _____	10. saturate _____	14. subject _____
3. realize _____	7. composition _____	11. advice _____	15. improve _____
4. exercise _____	8. prove _____	12. belief _____	16. support _____

1b Complete the questions below with one of the words from Exercise 1a. You may have to change the form of the verb.

1. She _____ the most divine music for piano.

2. You know, you can always go to your lecturer for _____ on how to write a good essay.

3. It's difficult to find mathematical _____ for every theory.

4. The food was completely _____ with fats, which were damaging to her system.

5. I've tried the new _____ and I STILL cannot lose any weight!

6. He doesn't _____ in ghosts.

7. I keep on speaking and trying to memorize grammar but my English still doesn't _____ .

> EXAM PREPARATION TASKS

1 Circle the letter of the best answer.

1. What was the only appreciable difference found between the two groups in this study?

   A. Women who ate the low-fat diet lost more weight.

   B. Women who ate the low-fat diet had lower levels of LDL cholesterol.

   C. Woman who ate the higher-fat diet ate a lot more carbohydrates.

   D. Women who ate the higher-fat diet had slightly higher blood glucose levels.

2. What does the article say about the Mediterranean Diet?

   A. The Mediterranean Diet is a no-fat diet.

   B. The study showed that it did not help people reduce the risk of diseases.

   C. This diet eliminates only certain kinds of fats.

   D. It could help people prevent heart attacks.

2 Match the facts with the researchers from the article. Write the letter of the items under the people for whom the statement is true. Two choices will not be used.

Dr. Jules Hirsch	A. promotes low-fat diets
•	B. made studying the effects of diets on health a primary field of study
•	
	C. believes people get fat by eating too many carbohydrates
Dr. Dean Ornish	D. worked on the largest study about low-fat diets and diseases
•	E. feels we need to continue gathering information about how to make people healthy
•	
	F. believes the study wasn't long enough
Barbara Howard	G. believes chronic diseases are caused by factors other than what we eat
•	
•	H. believes the study is invalid because it only studied women

> DISCUSSION PROMPTS

1. Do you believe the results of the study? Why or why not?

2. Do you think that diets work? Give examples (e.g., a low-fat diet; the Atkins diet; etc.). Prepare notes giving evidence or arguments for and against and then draw a conclusion. Compare your notes with a partner.

3. What could the government do to help encourage people to choose a healthier lifestyle? Do "federal guidelines" work?

BUSINESS

1 > THE BUSINESS SECTION

The business section of a newspaper looks at a wide range of areas: company news, business scandals, successful new products, economic news, mergers and takeovers, how developments in new technology affect companies and so on. The section in the *International Herald Tribune* called "Marketplace" carries news on global stock markets, share prices, and areas such as commodities and bonds.

1 **How interested in business are you?** Do you read these sections of the newspaper in your own language? Has anything interesting or significant happened in the business world recently?

2 > THE ARTICLES

In this section, you will read four articles related to the business field. Read the article headlines below:

Music business finds little to sing about

Spotlight: A wedding planner for a new Japan

Cross-cultural training: How much difference does it really make?

The beauty premium: Why good looks pay

2 **Write down how you think these headlines will relate to the topic of business.** Discuss your ideas with a partner.

1. _____

_____

_____

_____

2. _____

_____

_____

_____

3. _____

_____

_____

_____

4. _____

_____

_____

3 > KEY VOCABULARY

Below are some of the key words and expressions from the four articles in this section. Do you know the meaning of these words? Use a dictionary if necessary.

> marketing campaign
> retail sales
> market share
> to boom
> turnaround in sales
> business competency
> stagnant
> entrepreneur
> résumé

4 > USING THE IHT WEB SITE

4a **Go to the IHT Web site at www.iht.com and click on "Business."** Find an article in today's business news which interests you and write the headline below. Read the article and note the key idea(s). Check any key vocabulary in your dictionary.

_____

_____

_____

_____

_____

_____

_____

_____

_____

_____

_____

4b **Do you recognize the terms below?** What are they?

Dax	FTSE	Nikkei	Nasdaq

Music business finds little to sing about

> PRE-READING TASKS

1 **With a partner, discuss what type of music you like to listen to.**

2 **How do you listen to music?** (See the box below.) Have your music-buying habits changed over the years?

audio cassette	CD	MP3 player
on computer	mobile phone	other (specify)

3 **Link the following phrases with their definitions.** The first one has been done for you. What do you know about each term?

1. file-sharing networks
2. music download
3. anti-trust laws
4. online music store
5. subscription service
6. peer-to-peer

a. taking a song from the Internet to a computer

b. selling something where the user pays a fee up front

c. computer to computer

d. Internet service that sells music on a per-song basis

e. program which makes files available to others across the Internet

f. laws used by the government to break up monopolies

> READING FOCUS

Focus on the newspaper: STATISTICS AND FIGURES

Newspaper articles often contain many statistics and figures. Understanding these is vital to understanding the text.

1 **What do you know about the music industry?** Complete the following sentences by choosing the correct figure:

1. Apple now has more than (50% / 60% / 70%) of the digital music market.

2. Only about (5% / 15% / 25%) of Internet users have bought music online.

3. There are now at least (5 / 8 / 10) different ways of acquiring digital music.

4. iTunes is the (first / second / third) -ranking online music store in France and Germany.

5. (Three / Four / Five) record companies dominate the music industry.

6. The price of music on mobile phones can reach (£3.50 / £4.00 / £4.50) a hit.

2 **Now scan the article and check your answers.** Are you surprised by any of the figures?

Music business finds little to sing about

By Victoria Shannon

1 The global music business shrank by another couple of billion dollars in revenue last year, bringing the decline over the past five years to about 20 percent, the chairman of an international recording industry group estimated on Sunday.

2 Retail sales fell below $31 billion in 2005 from $33.6 billion in 2004 and $39.7 billion in 2000, said the official, John Kennedy, who heads the International Federation of the Phonographic Industry. Although music revenue via computers and mobile phones[1] nearly tripled last year to $1.1 billion, the gains could not match the decline in sales of CDs of recorded music.

3 Kennedy also said he did not expect a turnaround in sales this year, in part because of the effect of billions of songs traded freely each month over unlicensed file-sharing networks on the Internet. But he insisted that online transactions, which accounted for a robust 6 percent of the recording industry's sales in 2005, up from virtually nothing two years ago, would lead to a "bigger pie" by 2007.

4 Many executives meeting here returned again and again to three possible ways out of music's malaise: using the online price of music as a marketing tool to charge more for, say, a hot single and less for a golden oldie; making digital music formats standard and playable no matter what the device of the end user; and increasing music sales over mobile phones.

5 The first two approaches are direct stabs at Apple Computer and its tight grip on Internet music sales, with a market share of more than 70 percent last year. Apple set the bar at 99 cents a single when iTunes began in 2003, and Steve Jobs, Apple's chief executive, has continued to say that the simplicity of his pricing structure is still important in pulling in potential music customers.

6 Even Kennedy conceded that the digital market still needs coddling, with only about 15 percent of Internet users ever having bought music online—even though there are now at least 10 different ways of acquiring digital music, from buying ring tones on a cell phone to downloading music videos from the Web.

7 While Americans may be conditioned to expect a single song for their dollar, Gabriel Levy, head of music for RealNetworks Europe, argued that Europeans are already seeing price elasticity.

8 Levy, whose company runs the music subscription service Rhapsody, said that since iTunes is only the third-ranking online music store in countries like France and Germany, dominant Internet merchants in those places have found it easier to break out of the 99-euro-cent mold.

9 Pricing is an especially sensitive topic these days. The New York State attorney general is reportedly investigating whether the four record companies that dominate the industry have violated antitrust laws in the pricing of songs that are sold by Internet music services.

10 And the European Commission has looked into Apple's pricing in Britain, where it charges 79 pence, or $1.40, per track, compared with 99 euro cents, or $1.20, in France and Germany. Britons are also barred from downloading songs from the Continental music sites.

11 The price of music on mobile phones—up to £4.50 a hit in some cases—is a concern for some industry experts as well, even though they say people are willing to pay more for the convenience of instantaneous purchases.

12 Apple was a target of the music industry because of its refusal to make its iTunes-purchased music compatible with players other than its iPods. The chairman of EMI, Eric Nicoli, said the dominance of Apple "doesn't concern me at all," adding: "It's early days. To talk about dominance this early in the game is short-sighted." He also insisted that price flexibility and hearing any song on any player were crucial to the industry's long-term success.

13 Both issues, Nicoli said, are likely to come to a head in the marketplace, ultimately determined by what the customer is willing to pay. "If the consumer is disappointed," he said, "that's a pity, because it's unavoidable. I think market forces in time will address it."

14 Free music sharing on the Web still tops paid downloads by thousands to one, for instance. In only two European countries out of five surveyed by Jupiter Research—Britain and Germany—do legal music downloaders outnumber the illegal downloaders.

15 In France, Spain and Sweden, there are more than twice as many music downloaders using file-sharing networks as those paying for their digital tracks. In Sweden, in fact, music piracy has turned into such a populist cause that a political party formed this year aims for laws to support so-called peer-to-peer networks.

16 A senior research analyst said: "It's a little difficult not to be a pessimist. There's so much work to be done to get this industry to the right place."

---

1. mobile phones: cell phones

> COMPREHENSION WORK

Read the complete text.

1 Trends

According to the text, decide if the following trends are **going up, down,** or **not stated.** Mark them {↑}, {↓} or {–}

global music business revenue from music downloads	online transactions CD sales music on cell phones	music video downloads

> VOCABULARY WORK

1a Match words from each column to create collocations taken from the article.

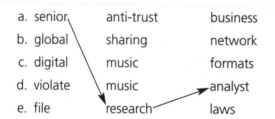

Noun–Noun		Adjective–Noun	
1. retail	a. forces	6. digital	f. transaction
2. pricing	b. piracy	7. online	g. tool
3. music	c. elasticity	8. marketing	h. music
4. price	d. structure	9. tight	i. purchases
5. market	e. sales	10. instantaneous	j. grip

1b Three-part collocations are common in business language (e.g., "international marketing manager" / "to organize a sales conference"). Match the words from each column to form 3-part collocations.

a. senior	anti-trust	business
b. global	sharing	network
c. digital	music	formats
d. violate	music	analyst
e. file	research	laws

1c Complete the following sentences below using a collocation from Exercises 1a and 1b above.

1. Many people believe _____ _____ is destroying the industry.

2. The web site has a safe system for processing _____ _____ .

3. They exchanged music over the Internet using a _____ _____ _____ .

4. He enjoys listening to _____ _____ on his MP3 player.

5. The company will change its sales strategy, due to the pressure of _____ _____ .

6. You need to keep a _____ _____ on expenses or you could find yourself in debt.

> EXAM PREPARATION TASKS

1   Complete the following sentences with prepositions.

1. The global music business shrank _____ another couple of billion dollars _____ revenue last year, bringing the decline over the past five years _____ about 20 percent.

2. Online transactions accounted _____ a robust 6 percent _____ the recording industry's _____ sales 2005.

3. Companies may have violated antitrust laws _____ the pricing _____ songs.

4. People are willing to pay more _____ the convenience _____ instantaneous purchases.

5. Hearing any song _____ any player is crucial _____ the industry's long-term success.

2   Circle the letter of the answers below that best complete the paragraph.

The Internet has changed the way we listen to music. Napster was an early program which allowed people (1) _____ songs with each other for free. The problem was that the artists did not receive royalties. After attacks from the entire music (2) _____, the free music exchange through Napster was shut down. What do the singers and bands think about (3) _____ issues? Many artists and record labels are campaigning to protect their (4) _____, and are against illegally downloading music. On the other hand, many people feel CDs are (5) _____ over-priced. Some feel that not enough money goes to the artists anyway and at least sharing music shows that people (6) _____ the art behind the music.

1.	A. exchanged	B. exchanging	C. to exchange	D. exchange
2.	A. industry	B. partnership	C. management	D. company
3.	A. this	B. their	C. its	D. these
4.	A. lawyers	B. candidates	C. knowledge	D. interests
5.	A. enough	B. greatly	C. too much	D. serious
6.	A. appreciate	B. appreciating	C. appreciation	D. appreciative

> DISCUSSION PROMPTS

1. Should people be allowed to share music across the Internet for free, or should they be sued? Do you agree with the current pricing of digital songs?

2. Is dominance of one product (like the iPod) or company (like Microsoft) good for business or inevitable? Justify your viewpoint.

3. Predict the future of the music industry.

Spotlight: A wedding planner for a new Japan

> PRE-READING TASKS

1 What does the expression "wedding day" make you think of? Write several words or phrases that come to your mind.

2 What kind of wedding would you consider ideal? Circle one word in each pair of adjectives. Discuss your choices with a partner.

elegant / simple	informal / formal
original / traditional	expensive / inexpensive
small / large	stylish / casual

3 Discuss these questions with a partner. Have you been to a wedding recently? What did you like about it? What didn't you like about it?

> READING FOCUS

Focus on the newspaper: KEEPING TRACK OF EVENTS

Events in a news story are often presented out of sequence. For example, a reporter often begins by discussing a recent event and then refers to earlier events to give background information or to explain what caused or led up to the recent event. To understand what happened and why, it's important to keep in mind the order in which things actually occurred.

1 Scan the article for time expressions. Write four more expressions with the paragraph number below.

eight years ago, para. 4

2 Scan the article to find when these events in Yoshitaka Nojiri's life occurred. Number the events in the correct chronological order.

_____ His wedding company rented fashionable restaurants.

_____ He was turned off by many of his friends' weddings.

_____ He was inspired by the film *The Warriors*.

_____ His wedding company built its own facilities.

_____ He made ¥1 million selling black leather jackets to teenagers in Shibuya.

_____ He decided to start his first business.

_____ He started a company to plan and create weddings.

Spotlight: A wedding planner for a new Japan

By Miki Tanikawa

1   Say the words "wedding day" to a Japanese bride, and a certain vision used to come to mind: big white dress, lots of relatives and friends and a rigidly choreographed, assembly-line ceremony in an impersonal hotel dining room, followed by a staid reception to which the boss was always invited.

2   A decade ago, as a young university graduate in his 20s, Yoshitaka Nojiri went to many such weddings. They completely turned him off.

3   "I would say to myself, 'I don't want to do that type of wedding,' and all my friends said the same thing," he said.

4   So eight years ago, Nojiri—a former teenage entrepreneur and collegiate rugby star who was working at an insurance company—rounded up ¥20 million, or $170,000, from investors and started a company to produce the type of weddings he and his friends did want to do: informal, party-style ceremonies, held in elegant surroundings.

5   The company started out by renting fashionable restaurants in Tokyo, then started to build its own facilities—country-club-like wedding "palaces" with large gardens and swimming pools. Nojiri and his staff also take on pretty much everything from producing the wedding to cooking the food and finding the bride's dress.

6   Today, Nojiri's company, Take & Give Needs, organizes 8,000 weddings a year and employs more than 600 people. For the year that ended in March, the company expects to post a profit of ¥3 billion on revenue of ¥33 billion.

7   The Japanese bridal industry, at ¥2 trillion in revenue a year, has been stagnant for the past decade. Take & Give Needs became a hit with young couples by putting the fun into weddings, making them more like parties than business events.

8   As recently as 10 years ago, Japanese weddings were family affairs where the bride and the groom had little or no control over the proceedings, and where omiai, or introductions arranged by the couple's parents, were still practiced. But as that custom faded and couples initiated their own matches, "there was a new generation of people who wanted something different and original," Nojiri said.

9   Analysts said the trend toward customization was true of Japan in general, as consumers turned away from the mass-produced goods and services that characterized the Japanese economy in the 1970s and 1980s.

10   Nojiri, 33, regards his talent as identifying undiscovered needs. "I formulate and turn into reality what people are mentally craving," he said.

11   His first business, started when he was 15, was selling black leather jackets emblazoned with school names and symbols to other teenagers in Shibuya, a popular youth enclave in Tokyo.

12   Nojiri, who fancied himself a fashion leader, was approached by clothing stores to help sell the jackets. Inspired by the 1999 film "The Warriors," about street gangsters in New York who wore personalized leather jackets like a uniform, Nojiri said he went to kids from different schools and said, "Let's do 'The Warriors' and hang out in the streets of Shibuya." He earned a commission on every jacket sold, pocketing about ¥1 million a month.

13   Partly because he is used to working for himself, partly because he comes from a frugal family—Nojiri is known as a penny-pincher.

14   As chief executive, he shares an office with four other people. Employees say he posts copies of telephone and electric bills on office walls with exhortations to economize written in the margins.

15   "I switch off lights before he arrives here," confided Megumi Shibata, 25, a wedding planner at a company facility in Shibuya.

16   Nojiri, who is still single, said his next step would be to start up a loan service to help young couples finance their weddings. The national average is ¥2.8 million, including the reception; a Take & Give wedding costs ¥4.3 million.

> COMPREHENSION WORK

Read the complete text. Are the following Japanese marriage and wedding customs old, new, or both? Write O, N, or B in the blanks.

1. _____ The wedding is arranged by a professional planner.

2. _____ Couples are introduced by their parents.

3. _____ Friends and relatives are invited to the wedding.

4. _____ The boss is invited to the reception.

5. _____ Couples have a customized wedding.

6. _____ Wedding ceremonies are often expensive.

7. _____ The wedding is held in a large hotel dining room.

> VOCABULARY WORK

LEARNING TIP: Compound nouns are common in English. In compound nouns, the first noun modifies or describes the second; in other words, it functions like an adjective.

1a **Find the compound nouns.** Circle two words in each set to form compound nouns with the bold words.

wedding	planner	affair	reception	bride	room
fashion	dress	industry	leader	party	family
university	generation	profit	degree	hotel	graduate
telephone	bill	star	jacket	company	school
business	deal	staff	consumer	event	restaurant

1b **Complete the sentences with one of the compound nouns from Exercise 1a.**

1. If you forget to pay your _____ _____ on time, they will cut your service.

2. Jake won't be home for dinner tonight because he has to attend a _____ _____ with his client.

3. A _____ _____ is someone who sets styles, not someone who follows the trends.

4. Julia finished college last year; she's the first _____ _____ in her family.

5. Bob and Jennifer decided to hire a _____ _____ to organize their reception.

2 **Word forms.** Write the letter of the correct definition next to the matching word in the middle column. Then find another form of the word from the article and write it on the line that follows.

a. introducing someone to something new	_d__ 1. customize	___customization___
b. beg someone to do something	____ 2. frugality	_____
c. not wanting to spend money	____ 3. proceed	_____
d. make something personal	____ 4. exhort	_____
e. go ahead with something	____ 5. initiation	_____

> EXAM PREPARATION TASKS

1   Circle the letter of the best answer.

1. The phrase "rounded up" in paragraph 4 is closest in meaning to which definition?

   A. gather

   B. make fuller or higher

   C. complete

   D. approximate

2. Which of the following is the best definition for the word "proceedings" in paragraph 8?

   A. a legal action

   B. a procedure

   C. an event

   D. a transaction

3. The word "faded" in paragraph 8 is closest in meaning to which definition?

   A. waste away

   B. grow fainter in color

   C. flourish with health

   D. disappear gradually

4. Which of the following is the best definition for the word "emblazoned" in paragraph 11?

   A. coated

   B. remembered

   C. adorned

   D. celebrated

2   Complete the sentences below with information from the article.

1. The younger generation wants _____ ceremonies, not formal receptions.

2. Take & Give Needs organizes _____ wedding a year, at the average cost of _____ each.

3. Nojiri believes his real talent is _____.

4. Nojiri's first business was _____.

5. The Japanese economy of the 1980s was characterized by _____ goods and services.

6. Nojiri says his next line of business will be a _____ service for young people.

> DISCUSSION PROMPTS

1.   Should young people have total control over their own wedding, without participation from their families?

2.   Agree or disagree with the following, and give your reasons: "People spend too much money on weddings."

3.   Imagine that you are going to start your own wedding planning business. What kind of services would you offer? Would this kind of business be popular where you live? Why or why not?

Cross-cultural training: How much difference does it really make?

> PRE-READING TASKS

1a **Write your own definition of the word "culture":** _____

1b **Compare your definition above with the four definitions below.** Which definition is closest to yours? Which definition is from the world of business?

1. activities involving art, music and literature
2. set of ideas, customs, skills, arts, etc. of a group of people in society
3. attitudes and beliefs shared by a group of people
4. "the way we do things around here"

1c **Which word does NOT form a collocation with the word "culture"?**

ancient	modern	intellect	corporate	company	business

2 **Look at the following terms connected with culture.** Match the terms with their definitions. What do you know about each of these terms?

1. cross-cultural training   a. studying the culture of one particular country (e.g., Japan)

2. sub-culture   b. a group of people with certain identifying characteristics

3. culture shock   c. training designed to teach people how to understand and relate to people from foreign cultures

4. culture-specific   d. feelings of disorientation when you experience a new culture

> READING FOCUS

Focus on the newspaper: DEVELOPING A STORY

Looking at the order in which a writer reports ideas helps you see how the writer is developing his or her point. What does the author emphasize in each paragraph? How does this contribute to the whole article?

1 **How will the article develop?** Match the paragraph headings below to the paragraph numbers.

1. The overall cost of cross-cultural training   _____

2. The benefits of cross-cultural training   _____

3. The dangers of cross-cultural training   _____

4. A memorable stereotype   _____

5. Which is best—theory or practice?   _____

6. The rise of cross-cultural training   _____

7. A couple looks back on the cross-cultural training they received _____

Cross-cultural training: How much difference does it really make?

By Gretchen Lang

1 Before moving abroad, Alecia Myers and her husband Ken drove to Chicago to attend a daylong cross-cultural training seminar designed to teach them how to understand and relate to people from foreign cultures. There they learned about high context[1] and low context[2] cultures, and sub-cultures, the seven dimensions of culture[3], and increasing intercultural business competency. One year later, happily settled in Austria, Alecia looks back favorably on her cross-cultural training and tries to remember what she learned.

2 "The thing I most remember is Austrians are like co-conuts and Americans are like peaches," she says smiling.

3 Cross-cultural and intercultural training, a marginal idea 30 years ago, has boomed into mainstream acceptance in the past 10 years with international businesses tapping into a large and sometimes expensive array of cross and intercultural training programs for their outgoing expat employees.

4 Supporters of cross-cultural training, and there are many, say that it eases the stresses of relocation, wards off culture shock and smoothes cross-cultural business relations. But even some intercultural professionals warn that the field is still unregulated and that trainers come from a wide variety of backgrounds. There are also those who question whether expats can really learn to communicate effectively with people of other cultures in one day.

5 Done well, expats say, cross-cultural training makes their moves easier, especially when it focuses on practical information about their host country. Done poorly, they add, it's a waste of money and time.

6 The study of global differences, once the province of social scientists and anthropologists, has made increasing inroads into the business community. International human resource managers are now deluged with materials advertising cross-cultural training seminars, videotapes, CDs, workbooks and Web sites. The number of vendors is estimated at more than a thousand worldwide, ranging from housewives with a few years experience abroad to academics with doctorates in "intercultural studies." In recent years, big companies like Berlitz and Prudential have added intercultural service divisions.

7 Fortune 500 companies now routinely purchase one- or two-day seminars at a typical cost of around $5,000 for an expat family. Some highly sought-after trainers can make $25,000 a day.

8 In its pure form, intercultural training seeks to teach people the knowledge, skill and motivation to communicate effectively and appropriately in a wide variety of cultural contexts.

9 But most intercultural trainers working with overseas assignees take the more pragmatic "cross-cultural" approach, combining practical information about the assigned country with comparisons to the home country. While clients are happy to have some intercultural communication theory mixed in, most say they want specific information about the culture they are about to enter and that they are most pleased with that aspect of the program.

10 "Culture specific is what they want," Bennet says, "and I don't blame them." Academics in the field complain that unless handled sensitively, such comparisons end up promoting cultural stereotypes like the peach and the coconut. While cross-cultural training is expensive for companies, some are finding that a failed overseas assignment is even costlier.

11 "It costs us from $150,000 to $200,000 a year for us to keep a family abroad," says Carl Burke, manager of Human Resource Global Services at Guidant Corp. "When you look at it like that, $5,000 is only a drop in the bucket."

12 Experts in the intercultural field acknowledge that the industry is still largely unregulated and companies and individuals wishing to buy these services should proceed with caution when choosing a trainer.

---

1. *high context: the context of what is around you is important in these cultures, e.g. how you sit, visual clues etc. Japan is viewed as a high context culture.*

2. *low context: surrounding context and visual clues are not so important in these cultures, so usually everything has to be said in a more direct way. The US is viewed as a low context culture.*

3. *seven dimensions of culture: refers to scales along which different cultures view the world (e.g., high context or low context).*

> COMPREHENSION WORK

1   Read the complete article and circle the alternative which comes closest to accurately reflecting the meaning of the passage.

1. Which word best represents Alecia's feelings on the cross-cultural training she received?

a. delighted   b. pleased   c. quite pleased

2. The writer mentions that intercultural trainers are, by and large:

a. under-qualified   b. over-paid   c. unregulated

3. On the whole, participants prefer:

a. theory   b. practical information   c. a mixture of theory and practice

> VOCABULARY WORK

1   Focus on adjectives and nouns.

1a   Transform the following adjectives into nouns, and vice versa.

Adjectives		Nouns	
Expensive	_____	Competency	_____
Unregulated	_____	Resource	_____
Failed	_____	Skill	_____
Social	_____	Stress	_____
Sensitive	_____	Training / trainer	_____
Effective	_____	Stereotype	_____

1b   Now complete the following sentences choosing with the word from Exercise 1a.

1. Sub-cultures are sometimes marginalized from the rest of _____.

2. Working and bringing up a family at the same time can be very _____.

3. Although he was regarded as a successful businessman, he felt his private life was a complete _____.

4. She's a very _____worker.

5. Trainers must be careful not to reduce people to a cultural _____.

> **LEARNING TIP:** A vital skill to develop is to deduce the meaning of new words from context. This will help you read articles quicker without looking up every word in the dictionary.

2   Guessing meaning from context. Look at the following expressions taken from the article. Match each one with its explanation.

1. mainstream (para. 3)   a. conventional

2. make inroads (para. 6)   b. very popular

3. sought-after (para.7)   c. practical

4. pragmatic (para. 9)   d. make progress

1   Write the correct answers to the following questions in the blanks provided.

1. Which paragraph tells the reader how much it costs to take a two-day seminar?
    _____

2. a. Where in the article can you find a definition of a high context culture?
    _____

    b. Write an example of a high context culture: _____

3. Which two paragraphs report what clients want from a cross-cultural training course?
    _____

4. a. Where in the article can you find a definition of intercultural training?
    _____

    b. Write the definition here: _____

5. Where in the article does the author list the different kinds of cross-cultural training available?
    _____

2   Circle the letter of the best answer.

1. What is the author's opinion about cross cultural training?

    A. It is useful for both individuals and companies.

    B. It needs to be specific and practical in order to be useful.

    C. It needs to have a good foundation in theory to be useful.

    D. It needs government regulation.

2. What is the expert saying in paragraph 12?

    A. Trainers vary in abilities, knowledge and price.

    B. Companies need to plan carefully before sending employees overseas.

    C. It is important to hire an expert that is acknowledged in the industry.

    D. Some kind of industry regulation is needed.

> DISCUSSION PROMPTS

1. A business visitor is coming to live in your country. Tell your partner five facts that would be important to cover in a cross-cultural training course for this person.

2. Have you ever experienced "culture shock"? If so, how? Discuss your experience with a partner.

3. If you were going to move to a completely different culture, would you go on a cultural-awareness training course?

The beauty premium: Why good looks pay

> PRE-READING TASKS

1   Write several reasons why beautiful people might have an advantage over ordinary-looking people. Discuss your reasons with a partner.

2   Check the statements you agree with.

☐ Beautiful people are more capable than ordinary-looking people.

☐ Beautiful people have greater self-confidence.

☐ Employers believe that beautiful people are more capable.

☐ Self-confident people appear more capable.

> READING FOCUS

Focus on the newspaper: REPORTING AN EXPERIMENT

When a writer reports the findings of a scientific experiment, it is important to explain to the reader the question being asked by the researcher (purpose), the steps taken to achieve the results (procedure), and the results actually obtained (findings). In addition, the writer should mention any measures taken to eliminate participant or researcher bias.

1   Scan the article to find the paragraphs which discuss the purpose, procedure, and the findings of the experiment being discussed. Write the paragraph numbers below.

Paragraphs

1. Purpose   _____

2. Procedure   _____

3. Findings   _____

2   Complete the sentences below in your own words. Refer to the article again if necessary.

1. The purpose of the experiment was to _____

_____

2. The researchers found that _____

_____

3. The researchers tried to eliminate bias by _____

_____

CD 1
Track 12

The beauty premium: Why good looks pay

By Hal R. Varian

1 Economists have long recognized that physical beauty affects wages, even in occupations where appearance does not seem relevant to job performance. It seems that attractive men and women are paid more than ordinary people for the same work. The question is why.

2 Two economists, Markus Mobius of Harvard and Tanya Rosenblat of Wesleyan University, recently reported on an experiment that tried to uncover the root causes of the so-called beauty premium.

3 Their experiment involved a labor market in which employers interviewed applicants for the job of solving mazes. Both the employers and the applicants had been recruited from a pool of students. The applicants first filled out a résumé describing their age, sex, university, graduation date, job experience, extracurricular activities and hobbies.

4 Then the experimenters gave the applicants a simple maze to solve.

5 After completing this task, the applicants were asked to estimate how many similar mazes they would be able to solve during their 15-minute employment period. This estimate was interpreted as a measure of the subjects' confidence in their own abilities.

6 Next, five employers considered the subjects for a maze-solving job under a variety of interview treatments. In some cases the employers could examine only the potential employees' résumés. In other cases, they used the résumé and a photograph; the résumé and a telephone interview; the résumé, a telephone interview and a photograph; and the résumé, the telephone interview and a face-to-face interview.

7 The potential employers used the information to form their own estimates of the number of mazes that the subjects would solve during their 15-minute job.

8 After the employers reported their estimates to the experimenters, the subjects solved the mazes as best they could and were paid based on performance.

9 To get an unbiased estimate of how attractive the subjects were, the experimenters showed the photographs of all subjects to a separate panel of students and asked them to rate the subjects of the experiment on a beauty scale.

10 Armed with the data from these experiments and surveys, the economists found, for one, that beautiful people were no better than ordinary people in solving mazes. But despite having the same productivity as others in this task, beautiful people were a lot more confident about their own abilities.

11 Being good-looking seems to be strongly associated with self-confidence, a trait that is apparently attractive to employers.

12 When employers evaluated employees only on the basis of résumés, physical appearance had no impact on their estimates, as one would expect. But all of the other treatments showed higher productivity estimates for beautiful people, with the face-to-face interviews yielding the largest numbers.

13 Interestingly, employers thought beautiful people were more productive even when their only interaction was by telephone. It appears that the confidence that beautiful people have in themselves comes across over the phone as well as in person. But even when the experimenters controlled for self-confidence, they found that employers overestimated the productivity of beautiful people. The economists estimated that about 15 percent to 20 percent of the beauty premium is a result of the self-confidence effect, while oral and visual communication each contribute about 40 percent.

14 As the researchers put it, "Employers (wrongly) expect good-looking workers to perform better than their less attractive counterparts under both visual and oral interaction, even after controlling for individual worker characteristics and worker confidence."

15 So perhaps beauty is a two-edged sword. If you are beautiful, people expect you to be better than ordinary-looking people, even in mundane tasks like solving mazes. But when good-looking people do not perform as expected, others feel let down. The rest of us can take solace in the fact that it is easier for us to meet expectations.

> COMPREHENSION WORK

Read the article and answer the following "why" questions. In some cases you will have to infer the answers, so different answers are possible.

Why...

1. did the researchers use students as both the employers and applicants in the study?

2. were five different treatments used?

3. were applicants paid to solve mazes based on their performance?

4. were photographs shown to a separate panel of students?

5. did employers have higher expectations of beautiful people?

6. did beautiful people do better in telephone interviews?

7. is beauty sometimes a "two-edged sword"?

> VOCABULARY WORK

1a **Focus on vocabulary used in scientific experiments.** Find the following words in the article and write an appropriate synonym or definition.

1. interpret (para. 5) _____
2. measure (para. 5) _____
3. subject (para. 6) _____
4. treatment (para. 6) _____
5. unbiased (para. 9) _____

6. rate (para. 9) _____
7. data (para. 10) _____
8. yielding (para. 12) _____
9. control for (para. 13) _____
10. perform (para. 14) _____

1b **Complete the sentences below with the correct form of a word from Exercise 1a.**

1. Approximately fifty _____ were enrolled in the study.

2. In the experiment on racial attitudes, the researchers _____ income level because they didn't want it to influence the outcome.

3. The experiment didn't _____ the results the researchers were expecting.

4. To everyone's surprise, the older men _____ better on the tests than the younger ones.

5. It's difficult to be _____ if you want an experiment to succeed.

2 **Find the words in the article with the following meanings.**

1. everyday, ordinary _____
2. a graphic puzzle _____
3. linked _____

4. possible, not actual _____
5. comfort, reassurance _____
6. giving good results _____

> EXAM PREPARATION TASKS

1   Check the boxes of the correct answer choices. Each question will have two correct answers.

1. Which two statements can be inferred from the passage?

☐ A. Ordinary people rarely disappoint others.

☐ B. Pretty people have higher expectations.

☐ C. Beautiful people tend to be more self-assured.

☐ D. The writer considers himself ordinary.

2. What are two reasons that employers pay beautiful people more money?

☐ A. Employers expect more from beauties.

☐ B. Beautiful people perform higher than ordinary employees.

☐ C. Self-esteem is a desirable trait.

☐ D. Beauty can add to overall job performance.

2   According to the information in the article, determine if the statements below are true, false or not given in the article. Next to the sentences write T, F, or NG.

_____ 1. To determine attractiveness, the researchers had the employers rank candidates on looks.

_____ 2. The participating candidates were paid to solve mazes.

_____ 3. Everyone was given the same simple maze.

_____ 4. About 40 percent of the beauty premium might actually be based on confidence.

_____ 5. Candidates guessed how many mazes they could complete in 15 minutes.

_____ 6. Employers guessed how many mazes the candidates could complete in 15 minutes.

_____ 7. The candidates filled in a form to ensure all their résumés were of a similar format.

_____ 8. The researchers tried to control the self-confidence variable in their study.

_____ 9. Beautiful people performed better on the maze task in the trial.

_____ 10. This research was conducted by economists, not psychologists.

> DISCUSSION PROMPTS

1.   Were you surprised by the results of the experiment? Why or why not?

2.   In groups, devise a different experiment to test people's attitudes toward beautiful people.

3.   The article says that employers may be "let down" when they see that their good-looking employees don't perform as well as expected. What other possible downsides are there to being beautiful? Discuss your answers with a partner.

LIFESTYLE

1 > STYLE AND TRAVEL

Two important sections in the *International Herald Tribune* are style and travel. The style section looks at the world of fashion and design. Many articles focus on the latest fashion shows in places like Paris, London, New York, Milan, and Tokyo. The latest collections from famous designers are mentioned, such as Giorgio Armani and Stella McCartney. These articles tend to have a short shelf life, as they are referring to this season's fashions.

The *International Herald Tribune* includes a regular feature on all aspects of traveling: budget airlines, hotels, the problems of traveling, the business traveler and so on. These articles are often interesting and include amusing anecdotes.

Look at the following headlines and mark them [T] for travel or [S] for style. Which articles would you be interested in reading?

The rhythmic blues of the Niger River

Highlights from the Paris collection

Black is back: The new season is about sobriety

Mexico's world heritage sites

Dressing for success: The new paradigm

2 > THE ARTICLES

In this section, you will read four articles. Read the article headlines below:

Retiring to cheaper climes? Caveat emptor

Cityscape: Street chef in a city that loves its food

The name game: Can anyone famous be a designer?

Stressed executives flee the pressure

What do you think each article will be about? Write down your predictions below. Discuss your ideas with a partner.

1. _____
   _____
   _____

2. _____
   _____
   _____

3. _____
   _____
   _____

4. _____
   _____
   _____

3 > VOCABULARY

Look at the following words. Transfer the words into the correct box. Can any words go in more than one box? You will find all these words in the articles.

pensions	labels	pressure	culinary excellence
food carts	a sabbatical	brands	savings
life expectancy	pace of life	stall	stressed out

Retirement	Food	Designers	Executive stress

4 > WHERE IN THE WORLD?

The first article you'll read is about retirement. Look at the photographs below which show some of the countries mentioned.

First, with a partner, discuss which of these places look the most appealing. Then, match each photograph to the country listed in the box below.

Canada	Jamaica	France	Thailand

Retiring to cheaper climes?
Caveat emptor

> PRE-READING TASKS

1 **Look at the photos below.** With a partner, discuss where you would most like to spend your retirement and why.

2 **Define the following nouns / noun phrases connected with living at home and abroad.** Use a dictionary if necessary.

utilities _____

tax breaks _____

relocation _____

a will _____

real estate _____

3 **At what age do men and women usually retire in your country?** Would you like to retire early? Discuss and justify your answer with a partner.

> READING FOCUS

Focus on the newspaper: PERSONALIZING A STORY

In order to engage a reader in an article, writers often start an article by introducing a person related to the subject. Although they are not usually the focus of the article, this technique personalizes the story and gets readers interested in the story.

1 **Read the first paragraph of the article.** With a partner, try to build up a picture of Lee Harrison and why he would decide to retire at 49 years old.

2 **Imagine today's main headline is** "Women to retire at same age as men." Using the technique described above, write the introductory paragraph to the article by introducing a main character. Think of the following when writing the text: name, age, career, family.

_____

_____

_____

Retiring to cheaper climes? Caveat emptor[1]

By Shelley Emling

1   After toiling for years as an engineer for an electric company in New York, Lee Harrison was more than ready for early retirement at age 49. On his modest pension and savings, such a dream would have been impossible in Manhattan. So after reading various guides on retiring to Latin America, Harrison moved to Ecuador, where the good life promised to cost a fraction of his former salary.

2   Harrison said he was enchanted by the country's pleasant climate, friendly residents, and by the fact that it is not yet overrun with expatriates. He recently paid $34,000 for a three-bedroom house alongside a river in Vilcabamba, a picturesque village surrounded by mountain peaks in the south of the country. The spacious home is a far cry from his small apartment in Manhattan, and he pays less than $10 a year in property taxes.

3   But not everything in Harrison's adopted home is cheaper. Electricity, for example, costs twice as much: 23 cents per kilowatt hour, compared with 12 cents in New York City. And although property taxes are low, so is infrastructure maintenance: roads and sidewalks, he said, are in poor repair.

4   With pensions dwindling and life expectancies growing, retirees like Harrison around the world are doing the math and concluding that moving to a lower-cost location will increase the chances of their money lasting longer than they do. In Britain, for example, at least one in eight people over 55 expects to be living somewhere other than Britain by 2010.

5   Americans like Harrison tend to migrate to Mexico and to Central and South America, where beachfront properties can be purchased for a smidgen of the cost of similar residences in Florida and California. Many countries, like Costa Rica, now offer tax breaks to foreigners who decide to retire there.

6   Britons and Germans continue to flock to Spain but are also going farther afield to places like Croatia, where an expansive seaside villa can be had for as little as $200,000. Even Japanese retirees, known for sticking close to home, are increasingly seeking to halve their living expenses by settling in Thailand and Malaysia. But real estate is only part of the equation. One has to feel at home in that bigger but cheaper house. And that, even for the most intrepid retirees, is where the wheels can come off the wagon.

7   A study of the top 10 retirement hot spots by the insurer Prudential UK found that 45 percent of Britons would like to retire overseas, with Spain being the most popular choice. But the study also showed that five popular retirement destinations were actually more expensive than Britain: Cyprus, Canada, Australia, France and Jamaica.

8   Experts in relocation and retirement, and the retirees themselves, point to certain areas that require particular attention before a move.

9   Retirees should set up standing orders[2] in a local bank account to meet bills and taxes. Failure to pay taxes could lead to court action and possible seizure of one's property. That is true in most countries, but falling behind in a foreign country becomes more of a headache due to language issues and nightmarish bureaucracies.

10   A key consideration when measuring quality-of-life expectations against available income is health care. Some costs might be covered by reciprocal health insurance agreements between various countries, although—as Americans know all too well—not all national health care systems are free.

11   While many seniors have their wills in order, the move to another country—and the purchase of property in that country—almost invariably triggers the need for a new will in that country.

12   Even if they wind up living lavishly on less money, some people just don't settle well in a foreign culture. Language may be an issue. Unmet expectations are also a risk. To avoid the disappointment—and the expense—of a bad move, retirees are recommended to spend at least six months in the new location before committing.

---

1. *caveat emptor: a Latin idiom meaning let the buyer beware*
2. *standing order: an instruction to your bank to pay a bill automatically*

> COMPREHENSION WORK

Read the complete article and transfer the relevant information into the grid.

RETIRING ABROAD			
Things to consider			
Benefits			
Drawbacks			

> VOCABULARY WORK

1 **Find the following words and expressions in the article and guess their meaning from the context.**

1. after **toiling** for years as an engineer (para. 1)	a. working hard	b. working a long time
2. a **modest** pension (para. 1)	a. adequate	b. small
3. **a far cry from** his small apartment (para. 2)	a. very different	b. slightly different
4. pensions **dwindling** (para. 4)	a. stabilizing	b. decreasing
5. a **smidgen** of the cost (para. 5)	a. large amount	b. small amount
6. living **lavishly** (para. 12)	a. in an expensive way	b. in a wasteful way

> **LEARNING TIP:** A metaphor is a type of comparison. The metaphorical meaning of a word or phrase develops from the literal meaning. An example of metaphor: in the phrase "he *shot down* my argument," the verb comes from the metaphor of war. Many writers use metaphors in order to make their writing more interesting or colorful in some way.

2 **Look at paragraph 6 again.** Re-write the words in bold using your own words.

Britons and Germans **continue to flock to Spain** but are also going farther afield to places like Croatia, where an expansive seaside villa can be had for as little as $200,000. Even Japanese retirees, known for **sticking close to home**, are increasingly seeking to halve their living expenses by settling in Thailand and Malaysia. But real estate is only part of the equation. One has to feel at home in that bigger but cheaper house. And that, even for the most **intrepid retirees**, is **where the wheels can come off the wagon.**

> EXAM PREPARATION TASKS

1   Fill in the blanks with no more than one or two words.

1. Which nationalities are retiring to the following places?

_____ are going to Central and South America.

_____ and _____ are headed for Spain.

_____ are retiring in Thailand and Malaysia.

2. Where is the most popular place for Britons to retire? _____

3. Name five popular retirement destinations that are more expensive than Britain.

_____

_____

_____

_____

_____

4. How long should a person live in a country before deciding to retire there?

_____

(Note: Write the correct units as you fill in the blanks for question 5.)

5. a. How much does electricity cost in New York City? _____

    b. How much does electricity cost in Ecuador? _____

2   Circle the letter of the answer choice that best restates the information in the italicized statement.

After toiling for years as an engineer for an electric company in New York, Lee Harrison was more than ready for early retirement at age 49.

A. Harrison retired from his engineering job after 49 years with the electric company.

B. Harrison enjoyed his job as an engineer in New York but felt ready to retire at 49 years old.

C. Harrison wanted to stop working when he was 49 years old because he didn't like his job.

D. Harrison thought it was too early to retire at 49 years old but the company got him ready.

> DISCUSSION PROMPTS

1. In many countries, there is not enough money in funds to pay out people's pensions now that life expectancy is so much longer. What is the situation in your country? What solutions can you suggest to this problem?

2. How do you measure "quality of life?" Compare your parameters with a partner. Which country or city do you think has a good quality of life?

3. What are your own retirement plans? Would you like to retire overseas? If so, where?

Cityscape: Street chef in a city that loves its food

> PRE-READING TASKS

1 **Think about your own experiences eating food sold by street vendors and answer the questions below.**

   1. How often do you eat food sold by street vendors?

   2. When did you last eat food from a street vendor?

   3. What kind of food was it?

   4. Was it cheap or expensive? How much did it cost?

   5. Do you think that street vendors should be regulated to ensure safety? Why or why not?

2 **What are your impressions of Bangkok, Thailand?** If you have visited the city, write a few things you remember about it. If you haven't been there, what have you heard or read about it?

> READING FOCUS

Focus on the newspaper: EVOKING A SCENE

Sometimes when reporters tell a story in a faraway or unusual locale, they use striking language to give the feeling of the place. They may use words relating to one of the senses (sight, smell, sound, touch, and taste) to describe the scene. This language helps readers more easily imagine the context of the situation being reported about.

1 **Scan the article for descriptions of these features of the Bangkok "cityscape."**

the weather	fast-food restaurants
the streets and alleys	Thai street food
the residents	the life of a vendor

2 **These words from the article relate to different senses.** Group them in the chart below.

aromas	sprawling	ginger-laced	serpentine
spicy	delicious	appetite	sticky
stillness	tender	sweaty	clack-clack-clack

Sight	Sound	Smell	Touch	Taste

CD 2
Track 2

Cityscape: Street chef in a city that loves its food

By Thomas Fuller

1 The world's great cities often lay claims to culinary excellence, but perhaps in no other place are the aromas and sights of food so ever-present, the residents so preoccupied with their next meal and casual conversations so frequently devoted to eating as in this massive, sweaty metropolis.

2 There are at least 43,000 street food vendors in Bangkok, the municipal government says, a legion of operators of food carts crammed into every available nook of urban real estate. Among them is Sompong Seetha, who for eight years has risen well before dawn to make his popular rendition of chicken rice, the specialty from the Chinese island of Hainan that combines tender boiled chicken with a spicy, ginger-laced soy sauce, served on a bed of rice and accompanied by a small bowl of broth.

3 "This is the only thing I know how to cook," Sompong said one day about 5 a.m., as he shoveled coals onto the lid of a giant cooking pot to steam rice.

4 Street stalls are the testing ground for Thai cooks, a Darwinian competition to win the hearts and sate the appetites of Bangkok's hungry—and often picky—10 million or so residents.

5 Sompong, 38, was trained to be a sticky-rice farmer in northeast Thailand, a life he left behind because it was not lucrative enough. Today, the serpentine concrete alleyways of central Bangkok are his adopted home.

6 Customers at Sompong's stall are served quickly, but this is not an anonymous fast-food experience. Although taciturn, Sompong connects with his clientele much more than the bored, pimply teenagers who stand behind counters at air-conditioned hamburger franchises do.

7 Sompong remembers his customers' preferences: dark meat or white. Some women forego the skin because they feel it is too fattening, he said. When he has not seen a customer in a while, he asks why.

8 Feeding his hundreds of loyal customers involves midnight trips to sprawling night markets, predawn deliveries, the clack-clack-clack of early morning vegetable chopping and the mixing and stirring of what Sompong calls his "secret sauce."

9 The near miracle of the process is that, for all the hustle and hard work, customers at his stall pay 30 baht, or 75 cents, for a full plate of chicken rice—cheap even by Bangkok standards.

10 Inexpensive but delicious street food fits into the mosaic of Bangkok's luxuries. To foreign tourists and wealthy Thais, this city represents cheap modernity: skyscrapers and swank hotels. Bangkok is the city of the hour long, $5 foot massage; the $2 air-conditioned taxi ride across town; and the $7 golf caddy, tip included.

11 When Sompong left behind his family's small rice farm nine years ago, he arrived at Bangkok's main train station without any idea of what job he would get. He worked for a year at a beef-noodle shop, earning the equivalent of $2.50 a day. But he wanted to own his own stall. So from an Indian loan shark he borrowed 30,000 baht, which at the time was worth $1,200, and started his chicken-rice business. Slowly he built up his customer base and paid back the loan—at 20 percent interest.

12 Rising at 3 every morning and working through the stillness of the Bangkok night is a lonely job. Even after the arrival of his assistant, Wilawan Kopaikaew, whom he pays $7.50 a day, there are so many tasks at hand—cleaning the chickens, steaming the rice, making the sauce, unfolding the tables—that the two exchange barely any words.

13 In the hierarchy of Bangkok food vendors, Sompong is a middling player. He leads a relatively comfortable life, earning about $17 a day, jogging every evening in nearby Lumpini park, going to the movies occasionally.

14 Sompong's goals are more modest. He would like to open a massage shop one day, but he will need to serve many more plates of chicken rice to meet that goal. His life savings, he said, is the equivalent of $2,000.

> COMPREHENSION WORK

Read the article. Then underline the errors in these statements about Sompong Seetha and correct them.

1. He has been preparing his rendition of chicken rice for ten years.

2. His recipe for chicken rice comes from Hong Kong.

3. He left his life as a farmer because the work was too hard.

4. He has an impersonal relationship with his customers.

5. His chicken rice is fairly expensive by Bangkok's standards.

6. He started his food stall right away after he came to Bangkok.

7. He rises at dawn every morning.

8. He pays his assistant $10 a day.

9. He leads a very hard life.

10. He wants to open a restaurant some day.

> VOCABULARY FOCUS

1a Find these adjectives in the article. What things (nouns or noun phrases) do they describe?

1. lucrative _____
2. picky _____
3. serpentine _____
4. anonymous _____

5. taciturn _____
6. sprawling _____
7. swank _____
8. middling _____

1b Write the adjectives from Exercise 1a after the appropriate definitions.

1. twisting and turning _____

2. choosy; difficult to please _____

3. profitable _____

4. average; neither at the top or the bottom _____

5. very luxurious or posh _____

6. quiet; not talkative _____

7. nameless; not special or unique _____

8. spreading out in all directions _____

2 Find four more words or expressions about food preparation from the article. Write the number of the paragraph in which the word or expression can be found.

chopping, para. 8

> EXAM PREPARATION TASKS

1   Circle the letter of the best answer.

1. Which of the following can be inferred?

   A. Sompong's family is from Hainan Island.

   B. The average price for lunch in Bangkok is 30 baht.

   C. Sompong is a very ambitious individual.

   D. Wilawan Kopaikaew makes a decent local salary.

2. Which of the following is NOT implied?

   A. Sompong created his own "secret" recipe.

   B. Thai people talk about food often.

   C. Fast food jobs are easier than being a street vendor.

   D. Sompong didn't have connections when he arrived in the capital.

2   Complete the summary below using words from the box.

aroma	culinary	forego	hierarchy	legion	lucrative
metropolis	middling	mosaic	preferences	preoccupied	rendition
sate	sprawling	serpentine	taciturn		

Bangkok is a large (1) _____ in Thailand known for its (2) _____
delights such as curries, noodles and seafood dishes. In this colorful (3) _____
of various street vendors is Sompong Seetha. Sompong considers himself a
(4) _____ individual but his customers would disagree. They find him
friendly and attentive. They buy his rice dish in order to (5) _____ their
appetites and to connect with someone in this (6) _____ city with narrow,
twisting (7) _____ streets. Even if you never converse with him, the
(8) _____ will reel you in with one sniff. Although not on the top of the
food vendor (9) _____, Sompong finds his place in the ranking with a
(10) _____ enough business to hire an assistant and lead a good life.

> DISCUSSION PROMPTS

1. Based on the information in the article, would you expect Bangkok to be an interesting city for a tourist to visit? Why or why not?

2. Because there are so many of them, street vendors in Bangkok are involved in a "Darwinian competition" to make a living. In your own town or area, where do you see evidence of this kind of competition? Is this phenomenon good or bad, and what kinds of effects can it have on a society?

3. Imagine that you are going to write an article describing the "cityscape" where you live. What things would you write about? How would you describe them?

The name game: Can anyone famous be a designer?

1a **The "celebrity quiz."** Who is who? Match the celebrity in Box 1 with a description in Box 2.

Box 1	Box 2
Jennifer Lopez	• Winner of 2002 Best Actress award at the Oscars
Britney Spears	• Once engaged to Ben Affleck
Sean "P. Diddy" Combs	• American rapper
Halle Berry	• British soccer player
Serena Williams	• Had a hit with "Oops, I did it again"
Eminem	• Tennis player
David Beckham	• Singer once known as Puff Daddy

1b **Skim the article and match the celebrities above to the product they endorse.**

perfume

watches

menswear

sunglasses

make-up

sports products

> READING FOCUS

Focus on the newspaper: FORMAL VERSUS INFORMAL

The subject of an article will determine whether the language used is formal or informal. Whether an article is light-hearted and informal, or serious and formal, the language used by the writer will reflect this.

1 **Scan the text.** Do you think this article is formal or informal? Discuss and justify your reasons with a partner.

2 **Look at the phrases below taken from the article.** Re-word these expressions using more neutral or formal language:

    1. the pros (para. 6) _____

    2. cool (para. 9) _____

    3. goes in for (para. 11) _____

    4. you can clap a name on anything (para. 14) _____

    5. steered clear of (para. 15) _____

The name game: Can anyone famous be a designer?

By Suzy Menkes

1   It is celebrity warfare. On Sunday, Jennifer Lopez, in a chiffon dress decked out with diamonds, joined the centenary celebrations of Coty—the venerable beauty house that has had a huge hit with the J-Lo Glow fragrance.

2   On Tuesday, Britney Spears fights back—taking over the giant billboard in Times Square to promote her first fragrance that is being launched under the auspices of Elizabeth Arden.

3   There is a neat symbolism in the idea that a pop diva should fill what has long been an iconic fashion spot, promoting Calvin Klein's jeans and any labels that want to make it in Manhattan.

4   Celebrities, having appeared in fashion's front rows and competed in the rarefied world of designer fragrances, are now moving onto the runways.

5   The proliferation of celebrity labels is a big story with an explosion of "A" list names attached to fashion lines. It seems that anyone in America can produce a collection—as long as they are already famous.

6   When Paris Hilton, Beyoncé Knowles, Lil' Kim or even Ivana Trump and her sold-on-television jewelry are in the audience, are they really there to promote their own brands—and maybe to pick up a few fashion tips from the pros?

7   J-Lo herself has a sports line through her Sweetface company. (Can Britney be far behind?) And there are upcoming licenses for J-LO watches and a footwear collection for spring 2005.

8   Leader of the celebrity pack is Sean "P. Diddy" Combs, who has parlayed his own personal swagger into a menswear business that is a genuine success.

9   Tie-ups between celebrities and sportswear are based on the concept of borrowed fame and cool.

10   "Urban" in America is usually applied to black music artists. They have been taken up in force by the fashion world, with Eve's "Fetish" label of sports clothes and active wear launched in Macy's last fall, while the raunchy Lil' Kim is producing a watch named "Queen B royalty."

11   Sports companies are interested as much—or perhaps even more—in men than women. Eminem now has a sportswear collection, while a genuine sports star such as the soccer player David Beckham goes in for product en-

dorsement, such as his Police sunglasses and other lucrative deals. Tennis star Serena Williams worked with Reebok and Diane Von Furstenberg; and Reebok forged deals with hip-hop's 50 Cent and also with Jay-Z.

12   And what about those fragrance and beauty deals? Britney's "Curious" with its rounded bottle and newly fashionable atomizer, is joining a big list of hits and failures. The cosmetic giant Revlon has used Halle Berry, Julianne Moore and Susan Sarandon. Lancaster signed J-Lo for a makeup line.

13   Clothing is an even more delicate balance, because there has to be a trained designer to interpret the celebrity's vision. And for all the product tie-ups and newly launched labels, New York's most revered retailers remain skeptical about celebrity brands.

14   "You can clap a name on anything, but we don't buy any of them," says Joan Kaner of Neiman Marcus. While Barneys' Gilhart says: "Our store customers are the celebrities."

15   Robert Burke, fashion director of Bergdorf Goodman, has steered clear of logos and celebrities.

16   "Our customer is very discerning and if a product is not good they will not accept it, whether it is made by a rapper or whoever," he says. "I think it is rather embarrassing of the fashion industry to embrace celebrity so much."

> COMPREHENSION WORK

Read the complete article and decide whether the following statements are true [T], false [F] or not mentioned [NM] in the article.

1. Elizabeth Arden celebrated 100 years as a manufacturer of beauty products. _____

2. Anyone can produce a range of designer outfits. _____

3. Celebrities are now taking part in fashion shows. _____

4. Sports companies prefer men to women in order to advertise their products. _____

5. Celebrities need trained designers in order to interpret their vision. _____

6. David Beckham's iconic status in the Far East makes him an excellent choice for advertisers endorsing their products. _____

7. Robert Burke is keen on using celebrities. _____

8. Launching a new sports line is easy for an actress. _____

> VOCABULARY WORK

1a Focus on adjectives. By using surprising adjectives, a writer can bring an article to life, making it more interesting. Look at the following adjectives taken from the article. Match them to their definitions below.

skeptical	designer	raunchy	lucrative	genuine	fashionable	delicate	discerning

1. Slightly rude and sexy _____

2. Potentially very profitable _____

3. Real _____

4. Up-to-date _____

5. Can differentiate between two things _____

6. Fragile _____

7. Not believing something to be true _____

8. Made by a famous manufacturer _____

1b Complete the sentences with one of the adjectives in Exercise 1a.

1. She was overjoyed when her company got the _____ new contract in China; it will make her a multi-millionaire.

2. The Rembrandt, which was thought to be a fake, in fact turned out to be _____.

3. Teachers have to maintain a _____ balance between encouraging the students and telling them about their failures.

4. She's a fashion guru—she only ever wears _____ labels.

> EXAM PREPARATION TASKS

1 Determine if according to the article the following statements refer to the people listed below. Next to each statement, write the initials of the person or people for whom the statement is true. The statements may be true for more than one person and each person may be used more than once.

_____ 1. has a designer fragrance

_____ 2. has a sportswear collection

_____ 3. is a fashion director

_____ 4. is marketing a watch

_____ 5. markets cosmetics

_____ 6. owns a menswear business

_____ 7. works for Revlon

JL Jennifer Lopez (J-Lo)

BS Britney Spears

PD Sean "P. Diddy" Combs

LK Lil' Kim

SS Susan Sarandon

MM Eminem

RB Robert Burke

2 Circle the letter of the best answer.

1. The term "decked out" in paragraph 1 is closest in meaning to

   A. a flat platform without walls or roof

   B. going out for the evening

   C. looking very similar to

   D. decorated with nice looking things

2. The term "parlayed" in paragraph 8 is closest in meaning to

   A. turn something into something better

   B. to hide or be ashamed of

   C. to be a leader of a group

   D. to wear well or look good

3. The term "runways" in paragraph 4 is closest in meaning to

   A. to leave home without telling people

   B. a beaten passage or strip of land

   C. a platform on which models walk

   D. a large designer shop

> DISCUSSION PROMPTS

1. Would you buy a product if it were endorsed by a celebrity you admired? Explain the reasons for your answer to a partner.

2. "You can clap a name on anything, but we don't buy any of them." Do you agree with Joan Kaner? Or, do you think a celebrity can make a good designer?

Stressed executives flee the pressure

> PRE-READING TASKS

1 **What are some common symptoms of "stress"?**

2 **Create sentences with the following words and expressions, which show their meanings:**

stressful (adj)

stress-free (adj)

STRESS (n)

(to be) stressed out (adj)

executive stress (n)

3 **Explain the following terms in your own words.** If necessary, use a dictionary.

backpacker	a gap-year	a sabbatical	golden parachute

4 **In your opinion, when is the best time in a person's life to travel?** Compare your answer with a partner and explain your choice.

> READING FOCUS

Focus on the newspaper: REPORTING SURVEY RESULTS

Surveys or *vox pops* are important in journalism as they identify an area of public interest. The story is usually written based on the results of the survey.

1a **Read the summary below about the findings of a survey of executives, asked about taking a career break.** Complete the summary with words in the box.

nearly	findings	81	precise	less than	large	over

(1) _____ 2,000 executives, 2,013 to be (2) _____, were interviewed this week to find out the best time in a person's life to travel. The (3) _____ of the survey were very interesting. (4) _____ half (49 percent) felt it was better to travel when you had some life experience, rather than as a student. But even as travelers, there were some items they couldn't bear to be without. A (5) _____ number of the interviewees, (6) _____ percent, said they would take their digital camera; but (7) _____ one fifth (18 percent) said they would take their iPod.

1b **Now scan the article to check your answers.**

Stressed executives flee the pressure

By Roger Collis

1   In my long-ago corporate days, when we were ruled by guilt, anxiety and card-carrying members of Workaholics Anonymous (two-ulcer men in three-ulcer jobs), the notion of a sabbatical, or time out, was a cruel joke. Sabbaticals were for tenured business-school professors, or for freshly fired vice presidents, floating down to earth on golden parachutes, or for the silver-haired rich with time on their hands. (Hell, we did not dare take our annual two-week vacation. You were stressed out and got on with it.)

2   Fast-forward to today with news that a wave of young stressed-out executives in their late 20s to early 30s has joined the 16 to 24 year-olds, who see traveling around the world in the "gap year" as a last chance to take time out before starting work, or before or after college—the "rite of passage" before settling into a career.

3   This is the finding of a survey of more than 2,000 British executives, aged 26 to 34, carried out by YouGov on behalf of the Bradford & Bingley building society, the second largest in England.

4   Nigel Asplin, group general insurance director at Bradford & Bingley, says, "Traveling has become increasingly popular at an age when life itself has become a 'stress zone.' People are using extended breaks to relieve work pressure. Having worked for a few years, they feel they deserve it."

5   Nearly half of 2,013 executives interviewed (49 percent) said they believe that the best time to travel is when one has some life experience, rather than during their student years; 46 percent see extended breaks as the chance to review their lifestyle and attitudes.

6   While this group would obviously have more money than students for travel, half still intend to do it in "backpacker" style, staying in cheap accommodation and having a daily food budget while still enjoying sports and cultural activities.

7   But there are some trappings of their affluent lifestyle they wouldn't leave behind: 81 percent would take their digital camera with them, 18 percent their iPod digital music player and 17 percent their Palm Pilot. Most popular destinations include Australia and New Zealand, Canada, the United States and South America.

8   Brett Shepperson, 32, left his job building a mobile phone network, leveraged his mortgage and, with the £25,000 ($48,000) proceeds, took off with his girlfriend for a year traveling around the world, spending an average of four weeks in each of 13 countries. They scuba dived in the Galapagos Islands, skied in Argentina and climbed the Cotopaxi Mountain in Ecuador. A high point was a Spanish language school in Quito, Ecuador, where they met a rich mix of people—teachers, executives, writers.

9   "I came back a different person, more confident, more laid-back, new perspective and mental well-being," Shepperson says. "I have a new job now as telecom project manager."

10   Fiona Smith and Justin Harvey gave up their jobs and a joint income of £60,000 to backpack across South America for six months, through Ecuador, Peru and Bolivia. Harvey, who has worked as an IT consultant in London for eight years, looks for respite and "a different pace of life" for a while.

11   I should be so lucky. I'll settle for a sabbatical long weekend.

> COMPREHENSION WORK

1 **Read the complete article and list as many reasons as you can find for taking an "extended break."**

- _____

- _____

- _____

- _____

> VOCABULARY WORK

LEARNING TIP: Phrasal verbs are composed of a verb and a particle. Sometimes, you can **work out** (guess correctly) the meaning logically (e.g. "She **came to** my house") but often it is impossible to work out what the combinations mean, even if you know the individual words (e.g. "She finally **came to**" = recovered consciousness). Phrasal verbs often have more than one meaning.

1a **What does the phrase in bold mean?**

I'll **settle for** a sabbatical long weekend.   settle for = _____

1b **Look at the phrasal verbs in the box below.** The top row has phrasal verbs used in the article. Find them in the article and try to guess their meaning. (Remember the verb may take a different tense.)

The bottom row has phrasal verbs that look like the others but have different meanings. Use a dictionary to find all the meanings.

settle into	give up	carry out	take off	come back	get on with
settle down	give in	carry on	take over	come to	get over

1c **Complete sentences 1–8 with the correct form of the phrasal verb above.**

1. There was a delay on our flight but we finally _____ .

2. You need to _____ what happened yesterday; stop worrying and live for today!

3. The concert was cancelled and so we just decided to _____ home.

4. I _____ smoking last week and I'm still feeling pretty stressed.

5. I'd like to stay on and _____ my duties for as long as possible.

6. His argument was so strong that I finally _____ .

7. He's always been a wanderer, but now he's finally _____ .

8. She lost her job when the company was _____ by their competitor.

> EXAM PREPARATION TASKS

1 Circle the letter of the best answer.

1. Why does the author mention "cheap accommodations" and a "food budget" in paragraph 6?

    A. to show approval

    B. to define a term

    C. to demonstrate changes

    D. to contrast two types of people

2. What reason do these young executives give for travelling now?

    A. They never had time to travel when they were younger.

    B. It is a "rite of passage" before they settle into a career.

    C. These trips provide them valuable new experiences.

    D. Traveling helps them to develop new perspectives.

2 Complete the related paragraph below using words from the box. Not all the words will be used.

anxiety	annual	attitudes	corporate	deserve
destinations	guilt	income	leveraged	lifestyle
mental	obvious	perspective	pressure	relieve
respite	sabbaticals	settle	ulcer	

Nowadays, more and more stressed-out executives are leaving their jobs to take extended breaks. These are not just the usual two-week (1) _____ vacations most people take each summer, but long (2) _____ that could last anywhere from a couple of months to a couple of years! They feel after working hard for a couple of years that they (3) _____ the time off. Their (4) _____ include Australia, Canada and South America. Now when you consider the average worker, it is (5) _____ that not everyone can leave their jobs for a year, but if you are confident that you can find a job when you return, why not go and enjoy a little (6) _____ in the sun? The stress and work will be waiting for you when you are ready to (7) _____ down to it.

> DISCUSSION PROMPTS

1. If you had an "extended break," where in the world would you most like to go? Plan your route with a partner and be ready to report back.

2. What three tips would you offer someone suffering from "executive stress"?

3. If you traveled, which three "trappings of an affluent lifestyle" would you take?

ARTS AND ENTERTAINMENT

1 > THE CULTURE SECTION

There is a culture section in the *International Herald Tribune* which covers areas such as arts and entertainment. This section offers up-to-date information on cultural events. Typical events covered include:

Movies	Opera	Classical music concerts	Rock concerts
Books	Exhibitions	Theater	

2 > MY PERSONAL TASTE

Before reading the articles in this section, think about your own preferences in the areas of art and entertainment. Why do you like a certain type of film or piece of music? Would you describe yourself as having a wide range of likes? List your own personal favorites below and then compare your list with a partner. Remember to explain your choices.

MY FAVORITE. . .	
Movie	
Director	
Piece of classical music	
Composer	
Song	
Singer	
Novel	
Writer	

What other areas of art and culture do you like?_____

3 > THE REVIEWS SECTION

The *International Herald Tribune* has regular reviews, typically of new movies and books. A useful reading skill is to be able to analyze a review in terms of its structure and content. Most likely, a reviewer will point out the strengths and weaknesses of a work, and evaluate it. Your "reason for reading" is usually to ascertain if it is worth going to the movie, or buying the book.

3a Understanding the adjectives used in a review will help you identify the author's viewpoint. Look at the following phrases taken from reviews. Are they positive (+), negative (−), or neutral (0)?

crowd-pleasing	outstanding	trivial	disappointing
lackluster	dramatic	impressive	eccentric
commercial	artistic	terrible	promising

3b Assessing a review

Find a movie or book review in the *International Herald Tribune* and read it. Decide the answers to the following questions:

• Was the writer positive, negative or neutral?

• Do you think the review is fair and balanced?

• Does the writer give examples to justify his or her opinion?

• After reading the review, would you want to see the movie or read the book?

4 > ARTS AND ENTERTAINMENT AROUND THE WORLD

4a Look at the titles of the four articles in the unit:

Portrait: A rising star in Chinese cinema

Swedes step ahead on ethnic harmony

Film: The audience speaks Spanish but not at the multiplex

A British invasion for the digital age

Before reading these articles, think about what you know about movies and music from these parts of the world.

4b Look at the box below. Can you name any pop groups or singers from these areas? Do you know any famous film directors or movies from there? Discuss your answers with a partner.

Iran	Turkey	America	Britain
China	Japan	France	Denmark
Europe	Latin America	Asia	India

5 > USING THE IHT WEB SITE

Famous people are often in the news because people like reading about them.

Go to the IHT Web site at www.iht.com and use the "Search" function to look for information on someone you like or admire. Click on the first result and skim the article. Why is he or she in the news? Did you learn anything new about this person?

Portrait: A rising star in Chinese cinema

> PRE-READING TASKS

1 **Think of a movie actor you like.** How would you describe that person to someone who didn't know him or her? Think of both the actor's physical appearance and personality. Write several words or phrases.

2 **Discuss these questions with a partner:**

Do you think acting is easy or difficult?

How do people learn to act?

Would you like to become an actor? Why or why not?

> READING FOCUS

Focus on the newspaper: REPORTING ON A CELEBRITY

Celebrities are often in the news because people are interested in reading about them. Interviews and news articles about celebrities often give the reader information about the celebrity's personal life. Sometimes there is no event to report—just being a celebrity is worth being written about.

1 **Scan the article to find information about actor Chang Chen's personal life.** Check the items that are true about Chang according to the article.

☐ shops at Eslite bookstore   ☐ uses improvisational acting

☐ skateboards   ☐ chooses parts according to scripts

☐ rides a motorcycle   ☐ would like to do more comedy

☐ is currently in love   ☐ plays sports

☐ gets top billing for his movies   ☐ plays video games

☐ plays pachinko   ☐ has an older sister

2a **How does the writer portray Chang Chen?** Find all the phrases or sentences in the article that give you an impression about Chang's personality.

2b **What impressions about Chang Chen stand out in your mind?** Without looking at the article again, complete these sentences.

1. Chang Chen is a _____ and _____ person.

2. Chang Chen is a _____ actor.

3. Chang Chen is a person who _____.

Portrait: A rising star in Chinese cinema

By Alexandra A. Seno

1 From an entire special display shelf at Eslite, Taipei's landmark 24-hour bookshop, Chang Chen stares, looking dangerous and intense, from the covers of a Chinese men's fashion magazine. A Japanese tourist says he reminds her of a young version of the late actor Toshiro Mifune, charismatic protégé of the great Akira Kurosawa.

2 In person, Chang is the kind of guy who arrives for a meeting at Nylon, a modern Chinese tea house, on a black, well-worn skateboard. His manager, Rachel Chen, who sat in on the interview, picked the venue for its proximity to his home and her office.

3 Given his savvy, his range of movie roles and the caliber of his Chinese directors, many Asian entertainment veterans believe that Chang will go a very long distance as a star. It is something observers have been saying since he gained international attention in "Crouching Tiger, Hidden Dragon" for his powerful performance as Lo, the nomad who becomes the lover of Jen, played by Zhang Ziyi.

4 Today, Chang is arguably his generation's top dramatic leading man in Chinese cinema. Especially for an actor of his age, his lineup of upcoming movies is impressive. Later this year, he will be seen as the star of the mainland movie about a Chinese chess living legend in "Wu Qingyuan" by Tian Zhuangzhuang, one of China's leading art filmmakers. Chang's Taiwan comeback, "The Best of Times," his first collaboration with Taipei director Hou Hsiao-hsien, will be in competition at the Cannes Festival next month. Chang gets top billing along with actress Shu Qi.

5 "Eros" is a trilogy of tales told by different directors, with Chang and Gong Li in "The Hand" by Hong Kong's Wong Kar-wai. (The other stories are by the American Steven Soderbergh and the Italian Michelangelo Antonioni.) Of his turn as a tailor enamored with a call girl, Chang says that the month working on "Eros" last year made him realize how much he loves his profession: "'Eros' for me is the beginning of my career and my self."

6 Chang said he felt transformed by portraying a man passionately in love yet unable to show it. "I started to think about what love is. Every day I went and I changed into my suit, stood in front of the mirror, fixed my hair. I got into the character and I changed. Acting became comfortable. It is a kind of magic. You must have the feeling; you must think it is real. When you feel you are acting, that is bad acting."

7 He laughs about losing money at pachinko parlors in Japan with Tian, a venerated figure in Chinese film, while working there on "Wu Qingyuan." With the eccentric Hou, Chang claims he found himself confused by the master's improvisational methods. They did one scene "five days, 20 times" with the actors not knowing the location of the camera. "It was terrible. Maybe I'm the kind of person who likes pain?"

8 While he chooses parts according to the script, he said it was never his intention to become known as an actor of art house productions. "I did a commercial film," he said, referring to the Hong Kong comedy "Chinese Odyssey."

9 "But not so successful," said Chen, who heads Wong Kar-wai's Taiwan operation.

10 "Commercial films are very interesting," Chang said. "But right now it is the last one. I hope I will have more chances. An artistic film I enjoy, but you can't get very good money." The niche he has made for himself, however, has brought in international product endorsement deals.

11 The dimples and the easy charm come out again when he discusses his off-hours. "I like to drink," he said, giving Chen a taunting look. She appears to be something of an older sister figure to him, and she squirms. After a brief silence, she volunteered: "He also likes to do sports. I haven't met him for two weeks, and all of a sudden he answers so spontaneously. I don't know what happened to him."

12 He grins. "I exercise. I like music. I play video games," he said, before pausing for effect and shifting his gaze back to her, "And I drink."

> COMPREHENSION WORK

Read the complete article to infer the answers to these *yes / no* questions about Chang Chen. If the answer cannot be determined from the information, write *Don't Know*.

1. Is he a formal person? _____

2. Is he a better actor than Toshiro Mifune? _____

3. Does he like to play challenging roles? _____

4. Is Hou Hsiao-hsien his favorite director? _____

5. Have his commercial films been as successful as his artistic films? _____

6. Does he enjoy teasing his manager? _____

> VOCABULARY WORK

1a **Focus on words ending in *-ing*.** Look at the *-ing* words in the sentences below. Do they function as nouns, verbs, or adjectives?

1. This article is fascinating. _____

2. Jane has always loved entertaining. _____

3. While they were arguing, their friends arrived. _____

4. Tom has been working on the computer all day. _____

5. Before answering, he thought a few minutes. _____

1b **Find five more words in the article that end in *-ing*.** Write the paragraph number and the function.

billing, para. 4, *noun*

2a **Descriptive adjectives.** The words below appear in the article. Circle those which are often used to describe a person. Then find how the words are used in the reading.

long	well-worn	eccentric	powerful
charismatic	international	commercial	brief
venerated	comfortable	entire	mainland

2b **Write the words from Exercise 2a which fit the following definitions.**

Someone who...

1. has strange or unusual habits _____

2. can easily attract followers _____

3. is highly respected by everyone _____

4. has a lot of authority or control over others _____

> EXAM PREPARATION TASKS

1 **Match the statements on the right with the people listed on the left.** Write the letter of the true statements *according to the article*, next to the people. Two statements will not be used.

_____ 1. Shu Qi	A. worked on a film by Steven Soderbergh
_____ 2. Rachel Chen	B. acted in the *Eros* trilogy
_____ 3. Zhang Ziyi	C. has an office near a Chinese tea house called Nylon
_____ 4. Akira Kurosawa	D. played a character named Jen
_____ 5. Tian Zhuangzhuang	E. wrote a movie about a Chinese chess legend
_____ 6. Hou Hsiao-hsien	F. is a master of improvisational methods
_____ 7. Wong Kar-wai	G. had an actor protégé
_____ 8. Gong Li	H. played pachinko with Chang Chen
	I. got top billing in *The Best of Times*
	J. has movie operations in Hong Kong and Taiwan

2 **Circle the letter of the answer that best completes the sentence.**

1. Chang Chen feels his most important movie to date is

   A. *Crouching Tiger, Hidden Dragon*

   B. *Chinese Odyssey*

   C. *The Hand*

   D. *The Best of Times*

2. Rachel Chen is obviously

   A. uneasy with Chang's drinking

   B. a fan of skateboarding

   C. trying to get Chang to do more commercial films

   D. in contact with Chang daily

> DISCUSSION PROMPTS

1. Have you seen *Crouching Tiger, Hidden Dragon*? What did you think of the story? the acting?

2. Are artistic films usually of better quality than commercial films? Can you think of an artistic film that became successful commercially? Which type of film would you rather go to?

3. Agree or disagree with this statement: "Anyone can become a good actor with the proper training."

Swedes step ahead on ethnic harmony

> PRE-READING TASKS

1a Read the following definition:

Ethnic: relating to a group of people who have the same culture and traditions

Do you agree with this definition? Is there anything you would add to this?

1b Look at the following words. Create sentences with each one to show their meaning.

ethnic diversity	ethnic origins	ethnicity
ethnic minority	multi-ethnic	ethnic roots

2 Match the terms below with their definitions. Is your own country religious or secular?

1. Kurds   a. religion based on the teachings of the prophet Mohammed

2. Islam   b. not religious

3. secular   c. someone whose religion is Islam

4. Muslim   d. ethnic group from Kurdistan

> READING FOCUS

Focus on the newspaper: REPORTING SOURCES

In a newspaper article, it is very common to draw on different "sources" to express a range of views. Writers do this in order to add credibility to what they say. It also helps them to build up a picture of his or her subject.

1a Read the following pairs of sentences and notice the differences.

a. Darin is the best young singer in Sweden today.

b. "Darin! He's the best!" said Hanna Osterberg.

c. The country is making progress in its integration of foreigners.

d. Analysts say the country is making progress in its integration of foreigners.

1b Which of the sentences (a–d) is a direct quotation and which is indirect?

2 Scan the article and find two more direct quotations. Who are they by? Consider *why* the author uses these quotations. How do direct quotes add to the feeling of the article?

Swedes step ahead on ethnic harmony

CD 2
Track 6

By Ivar Ekman

[1] Sweden's new king of pop is 18 and a heartthrob for the preteen set. The new queen is a 23-year-old singer-songwriter with a penchant for poetry. Both were enshrined at a recent gala for the Grammis, the country's most prestigious music awards. Both have roots in the Muslim world.

[2] The consecration of Darin Zanyar, born in Sweden of Kurdish parents, and Laleh Pourkarim, who arrived from Iran at the age of 8, is the latest manifestation of how immigrants in this formerly all-blond country are entering the mainstream.

[3] Zanyar, who sings dance pop and is known here simply as Darin, won the "best song" award last week for "Money for Nothing," a Michael Jackson-style tune sung in English. The Grammi was not a surprise: His catchy songs and boyish good looks make young Swedish girls go giddy.

[4] Pourkarim, or just Laleh as people call her, a long-haired brunette in the mode of folk stars of yesteryear, was named "best artist" for her poetic, guitar-based pop music. She has a broad following in Sweden for songs like her latest hit single, "Live Tomorrow," a ballad (again in English) about loneliness, broken dreams and hope.

[5] How profoundly attitudes have shifted here is evident in the fact that the religion of the two pop stars is not only not a hot topic, it is so far under the radar that the subject has not come up in the many interviews the two have given in this deeply secular country. And, despite the current intense interest in Europe and Islam, the origin of the two is of no apparent interest to fans.

[6] "Darin! He's the best!" said Hanna Osterberg, 9, outside her school in central Stockholm, adding, in a typical response among young people here: "He's a Kurd? What's a Kurd? Whatever, he's the best!"

[7] Like most Western countries, Sweden is struggling to adapt to a multicultural reality, and analysts say there are signs that the country is making progress in its integration of foreigners from different ethnic backgrounds.

[8] "There is a wave of young immigrant Swedes coming who are beginning to use art, culture and words to express themselves," said Zanyar Adami, a columnist for the newspaper Svenska Dagbladet who himself has Kurdish roots. "When this began, the establishment couldn't see past the surface: A writer with an immigrant background was always 'an immigrant writer.' What is happening now is that many are beginning to see past that surface."

[9] In some ways, Sweden has been more dramatically affected by immigration than other European countries.

[10] The first to arrive, during the boom years of the 1950s and 1960s, came from southern Europe. But in the last three decades, asylum seekers from further afield have dominated, with people flowing in from Iran, Iraq, Turkey, Bosnia, Albania, Chile and Somalia, among other places.

[11] Today, in this country of nine million people, the foreign-born population stands at 1.1 million, or about 12 percent, according to the Organization for Economic Cooperation and Development. While the proportion is comparable to the situation in the United States, it is greater than in France, 10 percent, and Britain, 8.3 percent, and nearly twice as high as in neighboring Denmark.

[12] "The change is bigger and has happened more quickly here than in most other countries," said Christer Lundh, a professor of economic history who has written extensively on immigration.

[13] To be sure, the changing demographics have created tension. Still, Sweden has largely been spared the violent ethnic confrontations that have roiled other European countries in recent years.

[14] While acknowledging that difficulties lie ahead, people involved in dealing with the new, multiethnic Swedish society look to the future with a certain optimism.

[15] As for Darin and Laleh, the pop stars, they have said little about their foreign roots. Darin says he is proud of his background, but does not think it matters for his music.

[16] "My music isn't Swedish, it's not Kurdish," he said. "It's pop, and that's universal."

> COMPREHENSION WORK

Decide if the following are true [T] or false [F].

1. The religion of the "king and queen of pop" is currently a hot topic in Sweden _____.

2. Sweden is adapting to its new multicultural reality _____.

3. The 1950s and 1960s were economically a hard time for Sweden _____.

4. Sweden, like many other European countries, has suffered violent ethnic confrontations _____.

5. Darin believes that his religious background is an important part of his music and his message _____.

6. Both Darin and Laleh are Grammi winners _____.

> VOCABULARY WORK

LEARNING TIP: Connotation refers to the "feelings" associated with a word. It is an important feature of English vocabulary. Words can sometimes have a positive or negative connotation.

1a Look at the words below. What connotation do they have? Write them in the appropriate box.

heartthrob	optimism	struggle	manifestation
prestigious	universal	confrontation	mainstream
immigrants	asylum seekers	harmony	proud

Very negative	Negative	Neutral	Positive	Very positive

1b Complete the sentences below with words from the box above.

1. The Oscars are the most _____ awards in the cinema industry.

2. Lennon sang "Imagine" in the hope that people would live together in peace and _____.

3. The number of _____ _____ rose dramatically after the genocide in Africa.

4. Many feelings, such as laughter and sadness, are _____—every human being experiences them.

5. Many immigrants are very _____ of their own culture and traditions.

2 The writer chooses to use certain words, expressions and metaphors to create a lively and interesting style. Why do you think the writer uses these particular words? Write your explanation.

Both were **enshrined** at a recent gala _____.

the **consecration** of Darin Zanyar _____

a **wave** of young immigrant Swedes _____

people are **flowing in** from . . . _____

> EXAM PREPARATION TASKS

1 Circle the letter of the best answer choice to complete the paragraphs.

How profoundly attitudes have shifted here is evident in the fact that the religion of the two pop stars has not come up in the interviews the two have given in this (1) _____ secular country. Despite the current (2) _____ interest in Europe and Islam, the (3) _____ of the two singers is of no apparent (4) _____ to fans.

1. A. deep	2. A. intense	3. A. root	4. A. interest
B. deeply	B. intensely	B. source	B. curiosity
C. deepen	C. intension	C. base	C. awareness
D. deepening	D. intentionally	D. origin	D. attention

2 Check the boxes of the correct answer choices. Each item will have *more than one* correct answer.

1. Darin and Laleh

   ☐ A. are Muslim

   ☐ B. are Kurdish

   ☐ C. received Grammis

   ☐ D. are King and Queen of Sweden

2. "Money for Nothing" and "Live Tomorrow"

   ☐ A. are love ballads

   ☐ B. are pop songs

   ☐ C. are sung in English

   ☐ D. won the "best song" Grammi

3. Immigration percentages in Sweden

   ☐ A. are proportionate to France

   ☐ B. are proportionate to the U.S.

   ☐ C. are eight times that of Britain

   ☐ D. are almost double of that in Denmark

4. Zanyar Adami

   ☐ A. owns the Svenska Dagbladet

   ☐ B. is Kurdish

   ☐ C. felt discrimination in Sweden before

   ☐ D. is a reporter

> DISCUSSION PROMPTS

1. Based on the descriptions in the article, which of the two singers would you prefer to listen to?

2. Describe your own country in terms of its ethnic mix. Which is the most "multi-ethnic" city you have visited?

3. Do you agree that "art is universal"? Give any relevant examples from different areas; for example: music, literature and painting.

Film: The audience speaks Spanish but not at the multiplex

> PRE-READING TASKS

1   Answer the questions. Discuss your answers with a partner.

   1. How often do you go to the movies?

   2. What kind of movies do you prefer (action, documentaries, drama, etc.)?

   3. Do you like foreign films?

   4. Do you ever go to film festivals? Are people who attend film festivals different from "regular" moviegoers?

2   Talk with a partner about a film you saw recently. What was it about? Did you like it? Why or why not?

3   What kinds of films do you think most Americans like? Why do you think these kinds of films are the most popular with American audiences?

> READING FOCUS

Focus on the newspaper: READING FOR AN ANSWER

Reporters sometimes write an article that begins with an implied or unstated question to which there is no immediate or obvious response. This type of article piques the curiosity of readers and encourages them to read carefully to find the answer.

1   Scan the article to find what group of people is being talked about. Circle the correct answer below.

   1. people everywhere who make Spanish-language films

   2. Spanish-speaking people who go to movies in the U.S.

   3. English-speaking people who go to Spanish-language films

2a   Consider the title of the article and the information in paragraphs 1 and 3. What is the implied question? Write it here.

2b   Scan the rest of the article to find the answer to the implied question. Write the answer, and the number of the paragraph where you found it.

Film: The audience speaks Spanish but not at the multiplex

By Charles Lyons

1 The sizzle from a showing at last month's Miami International Film Festival had not yet cooled, but Francisca Schweitzer, a first-time filmmaker from Santiago, Chile, was already coming to terms with the probable fate of her movie, "Paréntesis" ("Time Off"): like most films of Latin provenance, it remained unlikely to find a distributor in the United States, no matter what the festival audience might think. "It is a small movie from a small country," said Ms. Schweitzer, 31, as she sat on a beach chair behind the National Hotel here. Nevertheless, "Paréntesis" is a slickly made tale of a Santiago relationship in crisis.

2 Along with the co-director, Pablo Solís, Ms. Schweitzer flew to Miami as a guest of the festival, an event that has championed a new wave of Spanish-language films. She had hoped for a North American distribution deal following a favorable review in Variety and a warm reception not only in Miami but also at festivals in Toronto and Palm Springs.

3 To date, however, no deal has materialized, pointing to one of the more confounding puzzles of the film world: the expanding Hispanic population in the United States, which totaled 35 million in the 2000 census and is projected to top 100 million by 2050, still hasn't created a market for Spanish-language pictures.

4 "A prosperous Spanish-language market hardly exists in the U.S.," said Jack Foley, president of distribution at Focus Features. "The Latino market in the U.S. is not changing. Latinos most enjoy English-language Hollywood entertainment. They want escapism and entertainment, exactly as the majority of American moviegoers demand."

5 Mr. Foley said films like his company's Spanish-language feature "The Motorcycle Diaries" and Lionsgate's "Amores Perros," as well as IFC's "Y Tu Mamá También," had worked in the limited independent art market. But he added that they failed to attract the broad, multi-ethnic Spanish-speaking population in the United States because most Spanish speakers here don't want to see specialized films.

6 Similarly, the exhibitor Cinemark USA, which in 2002 began the film series Cine en Español in a Dallas theater,

found attendance to be lackluster. After less than nine months, Cinemark discontinued the series. "We just didn't have the numbers," explained Terrell Falk, Cinemark's vice president of marketing and communications.

7 Hispanic television, by contrast, has long thrived in the United States. Last year, advertisers spent over $3 billion on the country's top three Spanish-language television networks—Univision, Telemundo and Telefutura—according to TNS-Media Intelligence, which tracks advertising and marketing across print and electronic media. Moreover, popular telenovelas, like Telemundo's "Cuerpo del Deseo" ("Body of Desire"), can attract nearly two million viewers a night, according to data supplied by Telemundo, which is owned by NBC.

8 Now, a handful of companies are trying again to lure that audience toward feature films. Cinema Latino, a Denver-based chain that operates Spanish-language multiplexes near Denver, Houston, Dallas and Phoenix, for instance, is aggressively expanding its business, said Jared Polis, founder of Sonora Entertainment, its parent company. Mr. Polis said his theaters play roughly 80 percent first-run Hollywood fare with the movies dubbed or subtitled in Spanish. The remaining 20 percent come from Spanish-speaking countries and are screened in Spanish with no English subtitles.

9 "In the past decade, we have seen the success of Spanish-language media, television and radio," said Mr. Polis, who spoke by phone from Denver, "and we believe Spanish-language consumers, just as English-language consumers, want to experience the magic of the big screen as well."

10 For her part, Ms. Schweitzer lamented what she views as the American film business's narrow take on Latin films. "You spend three years of your life on your movie," said Ms. Schweitzer, "and an executive looks at it and quickly says: 'It's not a comedy, there's no blood. I can't sell it.' They see Latin America as a place with beautiful women, spicy food and exotic drinks. It's tough to get past that."

> COMPREHENSION WORK

Read the article. Then read the statements below and decide which are true for the Spanish-speaking population in the United States. Write T if the statement is true and F if the statement is false.

_____ 1. It's a large group that's growing rapidly.

_____ 2. They prefer specialized films.

_____ 3. They watch a lot of Spanish-language television.

_____ 4. They like the same kinds of films that English-language moviegoers like.

_____ 5. They don't go to comedies or films with violence in them.

_____ 6. They attend film festivals in large numbers.

> VOCABULARY WORK

1   **The following nouns appear multiple times in the article.** Find the words or phrases that are used to describe each.

1. market   _____

2. film(s)   _____

3. population   _____

4. media   _____

2a   **What nouns do these words describe?** Find the nouns in the article.

1. probable (para. 1)   _____

2. favorable (para. 2)   _____

3. confounding (para. 3)   _____

4. expanding (para. 3)   _____

5. lackluster (para. 6)   _____

6. narrow (para. 10)   _____

2b   **Match the words from Exercise 2a to the correct definitions below.**

_____ 1. poor, below average   a. probable

_____ 2. surprising   b. favorable

_____ 3. getting larger   c. confounding

_____ 4. positive   d. expanding

_____ 5. limited   e. lackluster

_____ 6. likely   f. narrow

> EXAM PREPARATION TASKS

1 **Match the people from the article with their opinions.** Write the letter of the opinion next to the person who holds it. One opinion will not be used.

_____ 1. Ms. Schweitzer

_____ 2. Mr. Foley

_____ 3. Mr. Falk

_____ 4. Mr. Polis

A. Spanish speakers want to see movies on large screens in the theater.

B. The only successful place to sell Spanish movies is on television.

C. Not enough people are willing to pay and see Spanish-speaking movies.

D. Hollywood is only interested in comedy, action or horror films.

E. The Spanish-speaking market in the U.S. is not changing.

2 **Circle the letter of the best answer.**

1. Which of the following opinions would the author most likely agree with?

A. With the rise in Spanish-speakers in the U.S., the demand for Spanish movies will increase.

B. Only the critically acclaimed Spanish-language movies can succeed at movie theaters.

C. Spanish-language movie makers would have better luck distributing to television instead.

D. Spanish-language movies need more violence and action if they want to be distributed.

2. Which would be the best replacement title?

A. Where are the Spanish-speaking moviegoers?

B. Industry baffled over the lack of demand for Spanish language media

C. The time for Spanish-language media has finally come

D. Spanish-language movies need to cater to the mainstream

> DISCUSSION PROMPTS

1. Agree or disagree with the following statement, and discuss with a partner: "Spanish-language films haven't been successful in the U.S. because there's too much competition from television."

2. Should Latin filmmakers ignore the U.S. and focus on marketing their films in Spanish-speaking countries? Why or why not?

3. The article suggests that the American film business is too market-driven. Do you think that the government should provide financial assistance to independent film makers? Why or why not?

A British invasion for the digital age

> PRE-READING TASKS

1 Talking about the music industry. Check that you understand the meaning of the following words and expressions.

record label	debut album	music piracy	a demo CD
independent label	talent spotting	copyright	music forum

2a Which of the following bands are British? Have you heard any of these bands?

Oasis	The Beatles	Abba	The Rolling Stones	The Doors
U2	The Arctic Monkeys	Blur	The Beach Boys	Pink Floyd

2b Do you prefer to listen to bands from the UK, the U.S. or from your own country? Explain and discuss your musical preferences with a partner.

3 Have you ever visited www.myspace.com? If so, tell your partner about your reactions to the site.

> READING FOCUS

Focus on the newspaper: FINDING KEY INFORMATION

Many writers put a lot of key information in the first two paragraphs. The remaining paragraphs are *amplification* and should include quotes, statistics or examples. The last paragraph should tie in all this information. It can, therefore, be a good idea to read certain parts of an article "intensively" and identify the important ideas, before reading the complete article.

1 Look at the following parts of the article: paragraphs 1 and 2; paragraphs 3–9 and paragraph 10. Decide whether this text conforms to the pattern described above.

2 Complete the Fact File below. Scan the article to find the missing information.

Fact File: Arctic Monkeys

Number of band members: _____

1. Formed in: _____, UK

2. Year formed: _____

3. First record label:_____

4. Debut album title: _____

5. Copies sold in first week of release (UK): _____

6. Product manager: _____

A British invasion for the digital age

By Eric Pfanner

1   The back story for the Arctic Monkeys is vaguely reminiscent of the Beatles—four lads from a gritty city in northern England—but the resemblance ends there. These youths are from the all-digital generation, born and bred on the Internet. For a business reeling from the effects of piracy and a dearth of successful international acts, a promising band like the Arctic Monkeys should be welcome.

2   Privately, however, some record company executives express a bit of ambivalence. Their unease stems not from the band itself but from the way it burst onto the British music scene. The Arctic Monkeys bypassed the record labels—for a time, at least—and used the Internet to help generate a following and to distribute their own music.

3   To some in the business, the experience shows how traditional functions of the record label—not just distributing CDs but finding and developing talent—are being changed by the Internet. Music companies are losing some control to specialists in online promotion, or even to the artists themselves.

4   "Bands have a much greater ability to get themselves out to the public, gain some sort of recognition and credibility and then sign with a record label," said Guy Moot, managing director of EMI Music Publishing, which owns the rights to the Arctic Monkeys' music. "The development part is also happening much more outside the record companies." Scores of musicians have recorded their own music and posted it on "social networking" sites like Myspace.com in the hope of being discovered. The Arctic Monkeys have demonstrated that they understand the power of the Internet they grew up with as a tool for communication and marketing.

5   The band was formed in 2003 in Sheffield, once the heart of the British steel industry but now, like many cities in northern England, a postindustrial capital of pubbing and clubbing. The band toured the region extensively, giving hundreds of live shows, plugging its Web site and giving away free "demo" CD singles.

6   On their Web site, the Arctic Monkeys also gave away full tracks of some of their songs and encouraged fans to share them with friends, an activity the music industry considers a criminal violation of copyright. They gained a following on British online music forums like Drowned in Sound, and word spread via sites like Myspace.com.

7   In time, "they had every A&R man in Europe chasing them," one record company executive said, referring to "artist and repertoire," the industry's term for talent-spotting. The Arctic Monkeys resisted until last summer, then signed with a London-based independent label, Domino, with the music publishing rights going to EMI.

8   The free downloads were then phased out by Domino, and the Arctic Monkeys began to look more like a conventional product of the music industry machine. Their songs found a place on British radio, building anticipation for the eventual release of their album, "Whatever People Say I Am, That's What I'm Not."

9   Jonny Bradshaw, product manager for the Arctic Monkeys at Domino says, "This great rock 'n' roll band . . . has touched a nerve with a lot of people." While Bradshaw attributed the band's success to old-fashioned virtues of good music, knowing the powers of online buzz may have helped, too. Weeks before "Whatever People Say I Am" was set to be released in January, its contents had leaked out on the Internet, and some in the music business suspect that was no accident. It sold about 360,000 copies in its first seven days, the best performance by a debut album in Britain.

10   Once a band has been discovered, the Internet is also playing a role in developing the relationship with fans, with firms that specialize in online publicity grabbing some of the action. They work with Internet music sites to plant stories about a band and can develop "viral" tactics—involving no conventional advertising—to spread the word.

> COMPREHENSION WORK

1 **Match the paragraph headings below with the correct paragraph in the text.** The first one has been done for you.

1. The new, digital generation   *Paragraph 1*

2. "Record sales"   _____

3. Everybody wants to be their label   _____

4. By-passing the music execs   _____

5. The times they are a-changin'   _____

6. A more traditional approach   _____

7. Net advertising for the fans   _____

8. Roots   _____

9. Word of mouth   _____

10. Self-promotion on the web   _____

> VOCABULARY WORK

1 **Find the following phrases in the article and match them to the most appropriate meaning:**

1. **plugging** its Web site (para. 5)   a. promoting   b. uploading

2. **violation** of copyright (para. 6)   a. breaking   b. condoning

3. **conventional product** (para. 8)   a. a popular product   b. a normal product

4. free downloads were **phased out** (para. 8)   a. limited   b. gradually stopped

5. online **buzz** (para. 9)   a. background noise   b. excitement

6. **has touched a nerve** (para. 9)   a. affected   b. upset

---

LEARNING TIP: Writers often deliberately choose words and phrases, which "rhyme" to create effect. *Alliteration* refers to the use of the same letters at the beginning of a word to create a rhyming effect.

2a **Re-word the phrases below, using phrases in the article.**

1. a hard, realistic city (para. 1)   _____

2. started and grew on the Internet (para. 1)   _____

3. going to bars and discos (para. 5)   _____

2b **Writers often create effect through their choice of vocabulary.** Look at the two phrases below. What effect do they create?

1. "invasion" (title)   _____

2. "burst onto" (the music scene) (para. 2) _____

> EXAM PREPARATION TASKS

1 **Put the following events in chronological order.** Write the letter of the events next to the numbers in the order in which they occurred.

1. _____   A. The band's songs were played on British radio.

2. _____   B. A music company tried to stop the free downloads.

3. _____   C. Different record labels wanted the band to join them.

4. _____   D. The band joined Domino.

5. _____   E. The Arctic Monkeys gave away free songs and publicized a Web site.

6. _____   F. The band formed and toured in the Sheffield area.

7. _____   G. The band released their album "Whatever People Say."

8. _____   H. Fans began to follow the band on British online music forums.

9. _____   I. The band's debut album sold 360,000 copies in the first week.

10. _____   J. "Whatever People Say" songs were released on the Internet.

2 **Circle the letter of the best answer choice.**

1. What can be inferred about the music industry?

   A. They don't like the Internet for business.

   B. They feel it is more important to tour than to put music online.

   C. They fear the Arctic Monkeys will be an international success.

   D. They don't want musicians to distribute their own music.

2. Which of the following is NOT true according the article?

   A. The Arctic Monkeys are a digital band.

   B. The band has an online following.

   C. The Arctic Monkeys had many record company offers.

   D. The band isn't giving away free music now.

> DISCUSSION PROMPTS

1. Morrissey, ex-singer of the Smiths, implied that one album is not enough to "prove" a new talent. How many albums does it take to become established? Give examples of established musicians.

2. Read the following phrase: "the Internet is a powerful tool for marketing and communications." Can you give more examples of this phenomenon?

TECHNOLOGY, SCIENCE, AND HEALTH

1 > TECHNOLOGY, SCIENCE, AND HEALTH

The technology pages in the *International Herald Tribune* examine areas which are radically changing the world around us, how we communicate and access information, and how we live. The science pages often analyze natural phenomena such as earthquakes, tsunamis or hurricanes or scientific discoveries. The health pages often examine recent discoveries and research about illnesses such as cancer. All of these articles contain information which will be of interest to the general public.

1a In this section, you will read four articles from the science, health and technology pages of the *International Herald Tribune*. Read the article headlines below and decide if the article is about technology, science, or health.

Is Internet auctioneer an arena for criminals?

Global warming: Adapting to a new reality

Fake malaria pills haunt Asians

Keeping in touch the blogger way

1b With a partner, discuss what you think each article will be about. Try to think of the key vocabulary you will need.

2 > KEY SCIENTIFIC VOCABULARY

Scientific articles often contain long scientific or technical terms. These are usually explained in the text. Fortunately, many of these words are similar across different languages.

Do you know what is studied in the following areas? Are these words similar to the words in your own language? Use a dictionary to help you if necessary.

anthropology	astronomy	biology	chemistry	climatology
ecology	geology	physics	psychology	sociology

3 > NEW WORDS IN TECHNOLOGY

New words are continuously entering the language. Many of these "neologisms" are scientific and / or technological. Many technological words have become common in our language. Look at the words in the box below. Have you seen them before? Do you know what they mean?

instant messaging	downloads	blog	wi-fi	chat
hacker	spam	hot spot	e-learning	e-book

4 > VOCABULARY FOCUS

Here are some key words and expressions from the four articles in the science, health, and technology section. Write them in the correct part of the grid. Check that you know the meanings of these words. Use a dictionary if necessary. Can you use these words?

auction	symptom	heat waves	merchandise
online journal	pharmacist	climate change	emissions
post (n / vb)	diary	fever	greenhouse gases
bid (n / vb)	drugs	vendor	e-mail

Internet auctioneer	Global warming	Malaria pills	Blogs

5 > USING THE IHT WEB SITE

Go to the IHT Web site at www.iht.com and click on "Health / Science." Find an article in the health and science news which interests you and write the headline below. Read the article and write a summary of the key ideas. Check any key vocabulary in your dictionary.

_____

_____

_____

_____

_____

_____

_____

_____

Is Internet auctioneer an arena for criminals?

> PRE-READING TASKS

1   **What is an auction?** Check that you know the meaning of the following words.

an auction	an auctioneer	to bid	a bid	bidder

2   **What do the following words related to law and crime mean?** Use a dictionary if necessary.

1. (to) fence _____
2. fraud _____
3. Internet crime _____
4. (to be) liable for (something) _____
5. to sue _____

3   **What is your experience using eBay?** Check any statements which are true for you. Then discuss your answers with a partner.

I have never used eBay ☐	I am an occasional user ☐	I am a frequent user ☐
I have bought items ☐	I have sold items ☐	

> READING FOCUS

Focus on the newspaper: OPPOSING VIEWS

Articles often give both sides of a story. Sometimes, the writer offers a balanced perspective, or argues the case for one particular side. Whichever focus they use, an argument must be supported, either by evidence or by a quote from someone who knows a lot about the subject.

1   **Scan the text.** How many verbs or phrases can you find in place of the verb "said"?

2a   **Read the following argument descriptors.** Match each argument (1–4) with its counter-argument (a–d).

1. Brozek implies that the plasma screens were not stolen, although the cost is low.

    a. eBay is anonymous, and is therefore a good place to sell stolen goods.

2. The writer mentions some fraud cases are quite high-profile.

    b. eBay may be liable for prosecution.

3. eBay is not a very good place to sell stolen goods, as people may recognize their property.

    c. The writer poses the question: were the plasma sets stolen?

4. eBay doesn't take possession of goods, so is unlikely to be prosecuted.

    d. The writer mentions some fraud cases are fairly ordinary.

2b   **Now scan the article and match the descriptors with their paragraph numbers in the article.**

1 _____ 2 _____ 3 _____ 4 _____ a _____ b _____ c _____ d _____

2c   **Which is the best description of the argument in the article?** Is it slightly biased against eBay, towards eBay or, on the whole, neutral?

Is Internet auctioneer an arena for criminals?

By Daniel Altman

1 When Duane Brozek heard the prices for his company's plasma-screen televisions on eBay, the Internet auction site, his first reaction was, "WowWEE."

2 One set that listed for $2,499.99 at Target sold on eBay for $1,550. Another model that retailed for $3,499.99 went for $1,925. Brozek, a spokesman for ViewSonic, stated his company did not know how the vendor obtained the supposedly brand-new sets or how they could sell them for those prices.

3 "I'm not implying that they have illegally left our plant," Brozek confirmed, "but whoever's selling those plasmas at those prices are selling them for considerably less than what we could sell them at."

4 Were the sets stolen? The possibility may not be far-fetched. As eBay grows, it is an arena for more criminal activity.

5 Some have achieved a high profile. A couple in Chicago sold about $3 million of allegedly hot merchandise on eBay before an investigation by the Federal Bureau of Investigation and local police led to charges last year.

6 But most cases are mundane, like the case of Kevin Mac Donnell. Four years ago, someone stole an 1836 first edition of Ralph Waldo Emerson's "Nature," worth about $3,000, from his rare book shop in Austin, Texas. Two years later, the book showed up on eBay.

7 "I contacted my local sheriff's department," Mac Donnell said. "I realized that he was a guy who had been in my shop two years before, just about the time that the book had gone missing."

8 According to Hani Durzy, a spokesman for eBay, the ability of victims to recognize their stolen property, was exactly what makes the company's sites poor venues for fencing. But Mac Donnell disagreed.

9 "You're allowed to do it anonymously, you can hide your feedback, you can have shill bidding," Mac Donnell said. "It's an environment that's almost perfectly designed for that kind of activity."

10 Another bookstore owner said cases of fencing on eBay were legion. "People complain almost on a daily basis that they've gotten ripped off, that they've inadvertently purchased stolen material."

11 Generally, he pointed out, allegations of fencing were difficult to prove, often coming down to one person's word against another's.

12 eBay's policy is firm: to prevent becoming involved in personal disputes, the company acted on suspected cases of fencing only after being contacted by police.

13 "We have to get direction from law enforcement, that they believe something is stolen and a report has been filed, before we can start looking for it," Durzy said. "It can never be pre-emptive, because we are not a law enforcement agency ourselves."

14 Durzy remarked that eBay never took possession of the items sold on its sites. As a result, he asserted, it was impossible for the company to check whether the items were stolen, or for it to sell stolen goods deliberately.

15 "Criminal liability requires the intent to commit a crime," he said. "We have never been sued in a case of stolen property."

16 Yet R.H. Helmholz, a professor of law at the University of Chicago, said eBay might still be found legally liable for facilitating a fence.

17 "I don't think that makes too much difference," he said of the company's role as only a virtual marketplace. "They're connected with the sale enough so that you could say they have participated in, and stood to gain from, dealing in stolen goods."

18 Durzy said eBay can confirm that about 0.01 percent of transactions conducted on its sites are fraudulent, involving goods that were stolen, not as advertised or never delivered.

19 With more than 300 million items listed in both the second and third quarters of 2004, even just 0.01 percent of transactions could amount to well over 100,000 fraudulent transactions each year.

> COMPREHENSION WORK

Read the complete article and complete the missing information about eBay.

eBay	
Three problems people might encounter when buying things on eBay	
Reasons that eBay should be prosecuted	
eBay's defense	

> VOCABULARY WORK

1a **Focus on adjectives and adverbs.** Study the lists of adjectives and adverbs taken from the article. Check that you know how to change the adjectives into adverbs and vice versa.

brand-new	virtual	illegally	inadvertently
mundane	fraudulent	anonymously	deliberately
		perfectly	allegedly

1b **Now complete the sentences using the correct form of the adjectives and adverbs above.**

1. Importing cocaine is _____.

2. Someone left an _____ note without a signature or any way of knowing who wrote it.

3. Life here is so _____ and boring—nothing ever happens.

4. It's difficult to do—in fact, it's _____ impossible.

5. I _____ turned off the firewall on my computer and was hit by a virus!

6. I think you did it _____—that was no accident.

> **LEARNING TIP:** A writer may consciously use informal language for effect. It is important to recognize these phrases in order to feel the full effect of the text.

2 **Formal and informal language.** Re-write the following phrases from the article using a more formal expression.

1. far-fetched   _____

2. hot merchandise   _____

3. to rip (someone) off _____

4. showed up   _____

> EXAM PREPARATION TASKS

2 **Look at the underlined pronouns in the sentences below.** Connect the pronoun to the word or phrase it refers to by circling the word or phrase and drawing a line between the pronoun and its referent.

1. (Brozek,) a spokesman for ViewSonic, said his company did not know how the vendor obtained the supposedly brand-new sets or how they could sell them at those prices.

2. eBay acted on suspected cases of fencing only after being contacted by police. "We have to get direction from law enforcement, that they believe something is stolen and a report has been filed, before we can start looking for it," Durzy said. "It can never be pre-emptive, because we are not a law enforcement agency ourselves."

3. Durzy emphasized that eBay never took possession of the items sold on its sites. As a result, he asserted, it was impossible for the company to check whether the items were stolen, or for it to sell stolen goods deliberately.

2 **Write the letter of the answer choice that best completes the sentences below.** Two choices will not be used.

1. A ViewSonic spokesman feels that the televisions may be stolen because _____

2. An eBay spokesman feels it is difficult to fence stolen items because _____

3. A theft victim feels it is easy to sell stolen items on eBay because _____

4. A professor of law feels eBay may be legally responsible because _____

     A. the company gained from the sale.

     B. the company recently lost some of its inventory.

     C. people are able to sell the items so cheaply.

     D. people sell things anonymously.

     E. people can identify items belonging to them easily.

     F. the company acts on cases if they are contacted by the police.

> DISCUSSION PROMPTS

1. Should eBay accept any kind of responsibility for criminal activities carried out?

2. In groups, decide on appropriate punishments for the following crimes:

    a. fencing   b. falsely describing goods   c. selling stolen goods

3. Can crime on the Internet be controlled? Consider specific examples, and brainstorm possible solutions with a partner.

Global warming: Adapting to a new reality

> PRE-READING TASKS

1a Look at the photos below. Have you recently read in the news about any examples of the natural disasters they depict?

Flood

Drought

Fire

Tidal wave

1b Have you, or anyone you know, experienced any of these? Discuss your answer with a partner.

2 What do you know about the Kyoto Protocol? Discuss with a partner.

> READING FOCUS

Focus on the newspaper: WRITING ABOUT NEW DISCOVERIES

Any discovery or new information has to be published with caution. Journalists must be sure all information is correct and that it is presented clearly and accurately.

1 Look at the following sentences. Although both of the underlined phrases are possible, which one makes a stronger claim?

1. The early warning signs of global warming are <u>apparent / unmistakable.</u>

2. Global warming <u>has also been linked to / is thought to be the cause of</u> recurring summer fires in Portugal.

3. Scientists say that global warming <u>may be partially responsible for / clearly influences</u> the rising number of powerful hurricanes.

4. Evidence of warming is now <u>irrefutable / considerable.</u>

5. Already, scientists <u>have been able to detect some hard evidence / call into question the presence of climate change.</u>

2 Look at the article. Which ones does the writer use?

Global warming: Adapting to a new reality

By Elisabeth Rosenthal

1   As countries across Europe reduce production of greenhouse gases in order to fight climate change, scientists and citizens are discovering that effects of warming are already upon us. Irreversible warming is already happening, they say, and will continue for a century even if polluting emissions are controlled by the Kyoto Protocol, the international treaty aimed at limiting greenhouse gases.

2   To this end, they say, governments and citizens must prepare for a steamier future, adapting to a climate that is hotter and stormier.

3   "In addition to mitigating climate warming, we should also be focusing on how to adapt," said Richard Klein of the Potsdam Institute for Climate Impact Research, in Germany. "In the last few years people have realized that climate change will happen. Adapting is not a choice—it's something we need to do."

4   The early warning signs of global warming are apparent: an increase in summer deaths due to heat waves in Europe; the northern migration of toxic algae[1] and tropical fish to the Mediterranean; the spread of disease-carrying ticks[2] into previously inhospitable parts of Sweden and the Czech Republic.

5   Scientists say that global warming may be partially responsible for the rising number of powerful hurricanes, like Katrina, as well as an increase in floods, like the ones that inundated parts of central Europe this summer.

6   Global warming also has been linked to recurring summer fires in Portugal, since the Iberian Peninsula has become hotter and dryer than in the past.

7   The role of global warming in creating any particular flood or fire or outbreak of disease is difficult to prove, since year-to-year temperature variability and other factors are involved. But the average number of yearly weather- and climate-related disasters in the 1990s was twice that of the 1980s, according to the European Environment Agency, in Copenhagen.

8   In response to this trend, countries and politicians are starting to think about changes they will have to make. French farmers are shifting to crops that better tolerate warmer temperatures—from corn to rapeseed[3], for example. Austrian ski resorts that can no longer count on snow are planning hiking trails and golf courses.

9   The Italian city of Brescia is supplying the elderly with air-conditioners, a rarity in that country. Planners of the new Copenhagen subway raised all structures to allow for a half-meter, or 1.5-foot, rise in sea level that they expect global warming to cause in the next 100 years.

10   Most scientific models predict that temperatures will rise from 2 degrees to 6 degrees Celsius, in Europe over the next century—slightly less elsewhere in the world. And people are largely unprepared.

11   Jacqueline McGlade, executive director of the European Environment Agency predicted that if nothing were done, people in northern and southern Europe, where the effect is expected to be greatest, would become "climate refugees," moving to the center of the continent.

12   Evidence of warming is now irrefutable, and almost all scientists believe it has been produced—or at least vastly accelerated—by emissions associated with industrialization.

13   Southern Europe is likely to heat up within the next two decades, the European Environment Agency predicts. Cold winters, which occurred once every 10 years over the last three decades, are expected almost to disappear, McGlade said.

14   Already, scientists have been able to detect some hard evidence of climate change.

15   With winter temperatures in Sweden rising by up to 3 degrees Celsius in the 1990s, many parts of the country have lost their winter snow and ice cover in the last two decades, producing dramatic effects on ecology.

16   Sometimes adapting to climate change is simple: The Swedish government is encouraging foresters to plant new species of trees that grow better in a slightly warmer climate, for example. In Hamburg and Rotterdam, new docks are being built to accommodate the likelihood of rising sea levels.

17   In other cases, adaptation would be so expensive that the authorities may opt to let nature take its course. Along the British coast in Norfolk and Essex, local governments are contemplating letting marginal coastal farmland, already beset by frequent flooding, simply sink into the sea as the water level rises. "The most sensible thing may be for man to withdraw and change the coastline," Klein said.

18   "You won't have to pay subsidies. And these fields could probably become a healthy salt marsh, rather than poor farmland."

---

1. algae: seaweed
2. ticks: small insects
3. rapeseed: plant with yellow flowers; used for making cooking oil

> COMPREHENSION WORK

> **LEARNING TIP:** Sometimes you need to read an article intensively and carefully. For example, the short abstract which precedes an academic article and outlines the content contains the most important information and should be read carefully.

1 **Read for details.** What problems are the following countries having? What solutions are offered?

	PROBLEM	SOLUTION
France		
Austria		
Italy		
Denmark		
Sweden		
UK		

> VOCABULARY WORK

> **LEARNING TIP:** Prefixes are common in English. Understanding how they work can be helpful in expanding your vocabulary.

1a **There are several prefixes that have the same meaning.** Find a prefix that means "not" for the words below.

1. The opposite of reversible _____

5. The opposite of refutable _____

2. The opposite of hospitable _____

6. The opposite of frequent _____

3. The opposite of responsible _____

7. The opposite of prepared _____

4. The opposite of expected _____

8. The opposite of likely _____

1b **Complete the sentences with one of the words from Exercise 1a.**

1. The illness is very advanced and I'm afraid, _____.

2. He drank too much and then he drove his car—this was extremely _____ behavior.

3. No one thought this low-budget movie would win the Oscar—it was completely _____.

4. Evidence of warming is now _____.

5. The tsunami was devastating—no one expected it and people were completely _____.

6. It is _____ that an earthquake would hit here; it's a very stable area.

2 **Vocabulary expansion.** Find words in the article which mean:

1. changing your behavior (para. 2): _____

2. poisonous (para. 4): _____

3. a plant or animal group (para. 16): _____

4. money to help pay for something (para. 18): _____

> EXAM PREPARATION TASKS

1   Circle the letter of the best answer choice.

1. Which of the following is NOT given as a sign of global warming?

   A. The movement of species into new environments

   B. The spread of disease to new areas

   C. The death of tropical fish

   D. The frequency of natural disasters

2. Which of the following is NOT given as a possible adaptation to global warming?

   A. Controlling animal species that have migrated

   B. Changing what is grown in an area

   C. Abandoning property

   D. Building new structures

3. Which country is changing their tourist attractions due to global warming?

   A. Italy

   B. Austria

   C. France

   D. Portugal

4. What does the author think about global warming?

   A. It needs to be reversed as soon as possible

   B. It cannot be fought against

   C. It is responsible for most floods, fires, and hurricanes

   D. It is primarily caused by gas emissions in Europe

2   Look at the passage again. Match the article's sub-headings below with the appropriate paragraphs from the article. One sub-heading will not be used.

_____1. paragraphs 1–3   A. Reading the Signs

_____2. paragraphs 4–7   B. Already Adapting to Changes

_____3. paragraphs 8–10   C. Letting Mother Nature Win

_____4. paragraphs 11–16   D. Controlling Global Warming

_____5. paragraphs 17–18   E. A Bleak Future

                                    F. Too Late for Reversal

> DISCUSSION PROMPTS

1.   Do you believe that global warming does exist as a phenomenon? If so, why do many scientists disbelieve it?

2.   What can be done about global warming? Make a list of three concrete suggestions for motorists, business people and citizens.

3.   Do you believe than mankind can ever resist the forces of nature, such as earthquakes, hurricanes, etc. Give specific examples to support your opinion.

Fake malaria pills haunt Asians

> PRE-READING TASKS

1 What do you know about malaria? Answer these questions:

   1. Is malaria fatal? _____

   2. In which part of the world is malaria most common? _____

   3. Which insect transmits malaria? _____

   4. What are the symptoms of malaria? _____

LEARNING TIP: It is important that when you record vocabulary, you try and store your words and expressions in "sense groups." This will help you to remember them better.

---

2 Divide the following words into three groups. Write them in the appropriate boxes below. Check that you know the meaning of all these words.

symptom	pharmacist	fake	counterfeit
laws	chills	treatment	cut-rate
purchase	killing	consumers	jail

CRIME	MEDICINE/ILLNESS	BUSINESS

> READING FOCUS

Focus on the newspaper: PLACES, PEOPLE AND INSTITUTIONS

Newspaper articles often contain a great number of names of people, places and institutions. It is useful to map "who is who" when studying a text, as this helps you later to process the meaning.

1 Scan the article for the names of the people below. Fill in the table with information from the article about each person.

NAME	INFORMATION
Ngeit Ngor	
Sombath Mao	a farmer from northern Cambodia
Kim Syon	
Dr. Jong Wook Lee	
Paul Newton	
Duong Socheat	

LEARNING TIP: Authentic texts often contain scientific or technical terms. Many of these are similar across different languages. It is often not important to understand these words to understand the meaning of the article.

Fake malaria pills haunt Asians

By Thomas Crampton

1. When the chills and fever struck, Ngeit Ngor knew his 14-year-old daughter needed drugs urgently. Like most farmers in this remote northern province of Cambodia, he and his wife both have malaria at least once a year, so the symptoms were clear.

2. "I went to the pharmacy to buy medicine," he said. "I did notice the package looked different, but didn't think it mattered." The pharmacist, Sombath Mao, a neighbor and friend, had purchased the drugs from a traveling vendor offering a cut-rate price.

3. Those pills were almost certainly counterfeits, made to appear like the real thing but worthless, and they are being blamed for hundreds of deaths in remote Cambodian villages.

4. The rising traffic, prompted by the increasing popularity of a costly new drug to combat an emergent and deadly variety of malaria, has authorities angered, doctors frustrated and consumers confused. The counterfeiters, who run small and mobile operations, are undermining the impact of what is considered a new miracle malaria medicine, *artesunate*.

5. Cerebral malaria is resistant to many other drugs and can prove fatal.

6. Kim Syon, the health center director in the north Cambodian town of Anglong Veng, said a spike[1] in the number of people seeking treatment for malaria—from a peak of 40 a month last year to more than 200 last month—may be due to the proliferation of counterfeit drugs that were not effective in combating the disease.

7. Fortunately, the fever that struck Ngeit Ngor's daughter was treated in time and subsided, but World Health Organization officials say the counterfeits that began appearing four years ago are now also turning up in Vietnam, Myanmar and Thailand.

8. "More severe punishments must be used against those selling these fake drugs," said Dr. Jong Wook Lee, director general of the World Health Organization. "The counterfeits of some drugs have nothing in them at all, while others may have enough ingredients to breed drug resistance."

9. The World Health Organization says malaria kills two people somewhere every minute, and the prospect of counterfeiters working against them in Southeast Asia and sub-Saharan Africa, where the disease has had many victims, worries experts.

10. "If these fakes reached Africa we would face an absolute humanitarian disaster," said Paul Newton, a malaria researcher with Oxford University working in Southeast Asia. "There is more malaria per capita in Africa than anywhere on earth, making it a potentially attractive market for counterfeiters."

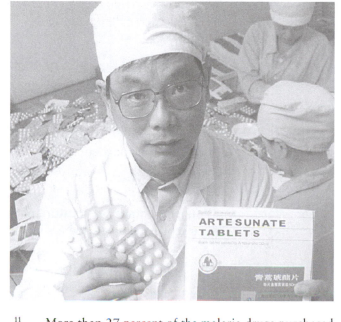

11. More than 27 percent of the malaria drugs purchased at rural pharmacies for a Cambodian government research project in May were found to be counterfeit.

12. "It's pure blood money," said Duong Socheat, director of Cambodia's National Center for Malaria Control. "The counterfeiters earn money by killing people."

13. Lax enforcement of Cambodia's few pharmaceutical laws and financial gain make the peddlers almost impossible to stop, he added.

14. "Nobody has ever been sent to jail for selling fake drugs in Cambodia," Duong Socheat said. "But there are easily hundreds of Cambodians who died in the last year due to the rising amount of counterfeit malaria drugs."

15. Developed from a traditional medical herb in China, artesunate is the most effective treatment for the cerebral malaria strain. A course of a dozen artesunate pills costs little more than $1, but that is five times the price of chloroquine, a formerly popular drug that has become largely ineffective against malaria.

16. The world's largest producer of artesunate pills, Guilin Pharmaceutical in Guangxi Province in southern China, says it has faced counterfeiting everywhere it exports in Southeast Asia.

17. Fake packaging similar to Guilin's boxes began appearing in Southeast Asia about four years ago. At first it was easy to spot: badly printed and covered with spelling mistakes. As Guilin introduced batch numbers and holograms that are difficult to duplicate, the counterfeiters quickly followed suit. The holograms on the counterfeit packages have become virtually impossible to distinguish from the genuine.

---

1. *spike: an abrupt, sharp increase in rates*

> COMPREHENSION WORK

1   Read the complete text and answer the questions.

1. How did Ngeit Ngor recognize the symptoms of malaria?
2. Who did the pharmacist, Sombath Mao buy the fake drugs from?
3. What is *artesunate?*
4. What happened to Ngeit Ngor's daughter?
5. How fast does malaria kill, according to the WHO?
6. Why would it be a "humanitarian disaster" if the fake drugs reached Africa?
7. Why is it difficult to stop the peddlers in Cambodia?
8. How can fake products be identified?

> VOCABULARY WORK

1a   Word formation is an important feature of English vocabulary. Complete the grid. Use your dictionary if necessary. Sometimes, there is more than one answer.

VERB	NOUN	ADJECTIVE
to enforce	_____	_____
to purchase	_____	_____
to counterfeit	_____	_____
to treat	_____	(un)_____
to fake	_____	_____
_____	frustration	frustrating _____
to effect	_____	(in)_____
to research	_____	____

Write the most useful words for you in your lexical notebook. Do not forget to mark the word stress. For example: to enFORCE

1b   Complete the exercises with the correct form of the word from Exercise 1a.

1. The disease is completely _____—but people have to have access to medicine.

2. He was given a painting, but it turned out to be a worthless _____.

3. It is _____ to see your goal and yet not be able to reach it.

4. The new president's policies don't work. They're completely _____.

5. As a scientist, he enjoyed working in the _____ and development section.

> EXAM PREPARATION TASKS

1   Circle the letter of the best answer.

1. According to the article, counterfeit malaria pills are:

    A. fatally poisonous.

    B. cheaper than chloroquine.

    C. produced in southern China.

    D. becoming harder to detect.

2. The primary purpose of paragraph 16 is to:

    A. show the cost of treating malaria.

    B. explain why chloroquine is so expensive.

    C. illustrate how drugs become ineffective against malaria.

    D. give examples of herbal cures of malaria.

2   Look at the following organizational representatives and their concerns. Write the letter of the organization's concern next to its representative. One choice will not be used.

1. _____ Director of a health center in Anglon Veng

2. _____ Director General of WHO

3. _____ Malaria researcher with Oxford University

4. _____ Director of Cambodia's National Center for Malaria Control

5. _____ President of Guilin Pharmaceuticals

A. The organization fears that technology is making it harder and harder to detect fakes.

B. Counterfeiters hurt the organization's reputation.

C. People seek help from the organization because they are given fakes at the local pharmacy.

D. The organization partially blames the government for not having more laws and regulations.

E. The organization fears the spread of counterfeits in Africa.

F. The organization fears counterfeits are causing resistance to legitimate drugs.

> DISCUSSION PROMPTS

1   Assign a suitable punishment for the following crimes:

a. The manager of a factory producing fake drugs _____

b. A worker in a factory producing fake drugs _____

c. Someone selling fake drugs _____

Discuss your sentences with a partner and see if you can reach an agreement.

2   "The main problem is the fact that drug companies in the West set too-high prices. They should sell cheap versions of medicine to the developing countries." Do you agree? Why or why not?

3   Should medicine be made freely available in a society, or should people be made to pay? Justify your view.

Keeping in touch the blogger way

> PRE-READING TASKS

1 **Read this blog about the experiences of an American living in London.** Would you want to read more information from this blog? Why or why not?

> We climb into Jean-Pierre's car, and take off, and immediately, all the cues I have been learning since childhood begin working against me. As far as my gut knows, the only time you have cars speeding towards you on the right side of the street is when you are driving the wrong way down a one way street. Plus, in England, you don't have to park in the direction of traffic, so many of the parked cars on our left are facing towards us as well. And my gut is further alarmed by the fact that I am sitting in the driver's seat but do not have a steering wheel, an accelerator, or, most alarmingly of all, brakes. Add in my lack of sleep over the past 24 hours, and you have the very definition of a nightmare ride. I'm glad we won't be owning a car here.

2 **What is your own experience of blogs and blogging?** Share your experiences with a partner.

3 **Which type or types of "blog" would interest you most?** Add any other types of blog which you are familiar with. Discuss your answer with a partner.

a personal diary	political	about religion
on business	on parenting	other (please specify) _____

> READING FOCUS

Focus on the newspaper: INTRODUCING A TOPIC

Sometimes articles introduce a new idea or product. To do this, the writer must give detailed explanations.

1 **Read the article as if this was the first time you'd heard of blogs.** Can you understand what a blog is from the article, without your prior knowledge on the topic?

1. What is a blog and where do you find them?

2. What makes blogs different from Web sites?

3. When did blogging begin?

4. How can someone create a blog?

5. How do blogs stay in business?

6. Why do people write blogs?

2 **Do you think the author did a good job explaining what a blog was?** What would you add?

CD 2
Track 12

Keeping in touch the blogger way

By Shelley Emling

1. Within a month of moving to London from Los Angeles in September 2002, Jacob Sager Weinstein started sending long e-mails to family and friends under the name "Jacob's London Diary."

2. "I had a few goals," Weinstein said recently. "Keeping in touch with family and friends was a major one. But I also wanted to preserve the memories of our experiences in this new country and maintain my writing muscles."

3. Then out of nowhere, Weinstein said, he began getting requests to be added to the distribution list from people he did not know—usually because someone had forwarded one of his entries.

4. The requests made him start thinking about broadening his audience. So in February 2004, he created his own blog at www.yankeefog.com. "I usually describe it as the adventures of a comedy writer in London," he said. Weinstein said the site attracted about 100 unique visitors a day.

5. Weinstein is just one of a mushrooming number of Internet users who are jumping on the blogging bandwagon, publishing online journals to write about topics that interest them. For expatriates, whose friends and family complain about "never hearing from them," blogs are becoming the answer to a knotty question.

6. Short for Web logs, blogs are little more than Web pages with postings that can be read by anyone using the Internet. Blogs generally can be updated easily, even by people with no knowledge of HTML coding[1].

7. Blogs also tend to be written in a more conversational tone than other Web sites and generally allow readers to post their own comments on the site.

8. When blogging began in the early 1990s, they were typically little more than the author's personal diary. But today blogs can and often do include photos and video, and the subjects range from politics to religion, business to parenting.

9. "In general I think blogging zeroes in on the human desire to be heard, to be seen and to be popular," said Shay Harting, chief executive of OnfuegO, a California company that helps create video blogs.

10. "It feeds the ego for many people," Harting said.

11. "I can't tell you how many people post a picture or video just so they are able to turn around and tell all their friends to take a look," he added.

12. Weinstein said that even a complete Internet novice could create a blog by using a site like www.blogger.com, where a person can make a few choices from a menu and, voilà, a free blog is created.

13. He said such sites generally put ads on the blogs that they help create, which is how they make money.

14. Weinstein said that if an author wanted a bit more control over a blog, it would take a little more know-how and money—but not much.

15. Two other blog fans, Freek Staps and his girlfriend, Claudia van Rouendal, created one just after moving from the Netherlands to New York last September.

16. "In the first place, it is mainly to keep our mothers up to speed," Staps said. "We've made it clear that our blog is for friends and family only."

17. "One thing we didn't expect," Staps added, "is that now people are using our blog as a way of keeping in touch with each other. So friends keep in touch through postings on our blog rather than through e-mail."

18. Van Rouendal added that to keep the blog interesting for friends and family, they sometimes post a picture of a celebrity they have spotted in New York City. Then ask if anyone can recognize the person and allow readers to comment on the photo.

19. American users of the Internet regularly visit blogs and the numbers are increasing, with 10 percent now reading them at least once a week, according to Charlene Li, an online media analyst in San Francisco with Forrester Research.

---

1. HTML coding: stands for Hyper-text Markup Language. This is the coding language used when writing text for the Internet.

> COMPREHENSION WORK

1 **Why do people keep blogs?** Look at the list of reasons below. Skim the article and then check which ones are mentioned.

1. As a way of keeping in touch with family and friends ☐
2. As a way of telling the world about disasters such as the tsunami ☐
3. As a way of getting published ☐
4. As a way of practicing writing ☐
5. As a way of feeling popular ☐

2 **Can you add any more reasons to the list above?** Were any other reasons mentioned in the article? Compare your answer with a partner.

3 **Has reading the article changed your attitude about blogs and blogging in any way?** If so, why?

> VOCABULARY WORK

1a **Guessing from context.** Read the following expressions taken from the article and guess their meanings.

1. **maintain my writing muscles** (para. 2)
   a. keep writing
   b. keep fit

2. **mushrooming number** (para. 5)
   a. numbers are maintained
   b. increasing numbers

3. **jumping on the bandwagon** (para. 5)
   a. doing the opposite
   b. doing the same

4. **a knotty question** (para. 5)
   a. a tricky problem
   b. an insoluble problem

5. **zeroes in on** (para. 9)
   a. negates something
   b. approaches something

6. **feeds the ego** (para. 10)
   a. makes people feel important
   b. makes people selfish

7. **know-how** (para. 14)
   a. knowledge
   b. ability

8. **keep up to speed** (para. 16)
   a. keeps them working quickly
   b. keeps them up to date

1b **Complete the sentences below with a phrase from exercise 1a.** You may have to adapt the expression.

1. The purchasers were as interested in getting our company's _____ as they were in getting the product itself.

2. She's always flattering him and _____.

3. We'll copy him in on any memos to _____ him _____ with the project.

4. He always agrees with the others—he just _____ when he joined that political party.

5. The number of jobless is _____ and the associated problems keep getting bigger.

> EXAM PREPARATION TASKS

1 **Circle the letter of the answer choice that best restates the information in the italicized statements.**

1. *The requests made him start thinking about broadening his audience.*

   A. Because so many people asked him to perform for a larger audience, he started thinking differently.

   B. He asked many people to join him because he wanted to show his work to more people.

   C. He started to open his mind to more ideas after he started seeing what people were asking him.

   D. He decided to address his thoughts to a larger group of people because people asked him to.

2. *In general I think blogging zeroes in on the human desire to be heard, to be seen and to be popular.*

   A. People like blogging because it allows them to be known by many people.

   B. People read blogs because it allows them to see and hear about many people.

   C. People want to blog in order to help themselves become more likeable.

   D. People who blog feel like nothing if they are not seen and heard.

2 **Scan the article for details.** Write short answers to the questions. Work as quickly as you can.

1. When was www.yankeefog.com begun? _____

2. What site mentioned in the article could even a new blogger use to create a blog?

   _____

3. How do sites that help create blogs make money? _____

4. Where is Forrester Research located? _____

5. What are TWO ways that blogs differ from most other Web sites?

   _____

6. What percentage of Americans read blogs at least once a week? _____

7. Where are Freek Staps and Claudia van Rouendal from originally? _____

8. What is the name of a California company that helps people make video blogs?

   _____

> DISCUSSION PROMPTS

1. "Blogging is quite vain and self-indulgent. Who really wants to read the ordinary ramblings of someone else?" How far do you agree with this statement?

2. How popular is blogging in your country? What do you think will happen on the Internet in the future?

The author and publishers would like to thank the following teachers for their invaluable input on this material during production:

Cally Andriotis-Williams	Newcomers High School, New York, U.S.A.
Sarah J. Brown	ITESO, Guadalajara, Mexico
Chiou-lan Chern	Taiwan University, Taipei, Taiwan
Pauline Cullen	Freelance, Brisbane, Australia
Sally C. Gearhart	Santa Rosa Junior College, California, U.S.A.
Victoria Gonzalez	Universidad Santo Tomas, Santiago, Chile
Pamela Humphreys	Griffith University, Brisbane, Australia
Kevin Knight	Kanda University, Chiba-shi, Japan
Paul Lewis	Perceptia Press, Nagoya, Japan
Luiz Otávio de Barros Souza	Associação Alumni, Brazil
Laura Sicola	University of Pennsylvania, U.S.A.
Nobuo Tsuda	Konan University, Kobe, Japan